Are You Okay?

The Carryover of Kindness

BY: A.S. DRAYTON

This book is dedicated to my children with love. I pray that it helps you somewhere down the road.

This book is based on my memories and is written from my perspective. I have tried to represent events as faithfully as possible, though some names have been changed in order to protect individuals' privacy. Common names/nicknames have been left as I remember them.

Credits
Edited by Charles Stewart
Art Design by Luce (Pedro Arias)

Special thanks to my wife, Neia, for supporting me during the entire writing process. Even when it required reading late into the night. I love you.

Thank you Denzel "Xavier" for your insight on memories that were foggy due to time, and for always being the Best Man.

Last, but not least, thank you to Anthony Lunan. This story would not exist without you.

Contents

Serendipity,
God's Hand, Happenstance, or Luck,
Which is your true name?

Are You Okay?
The Carryover of Kindness

Chapter 0

Serendipity

It was a typical Thursday night on a college campus, when I heard the words that would alter the course of my life forever. The grounds of George Mason University's Presidents Park were filled with freshmen; some could be seen congregating with friends in common areas to wind down from a hectic day, while others frantically searched for rides to parties around campus to drink and party the night away in complete disregard for classes the next day. I wasn't doing any of that.

That entire day, I refused to climb out of my bed which was the top bunk in my dorm. I would cry until I fell asleep, waking up only to stuff my face with gourmet delights from a heart shaped box of chocolates once my hunger pains became too gnawing for me to sleep through. Tears, sleep, hunger pains, chocolate. This cyclic experience was the culmination of a years-long emotional battle that had finally reached a tipping point. You see, the box of chocolates I was gorging on every few hours was originally meant to be a gift to my now ex-girlfriend who was the other half of the first relationship in my so-called "adult life", and my second one ever. But this wasn't about her. At least not really. It was about how I, Anthony Drayton, saw myself in relation to her.

With my head sandwiched between two tear-soaked pillows, I questioned everything I was doing with my life. *What am I now? What's the point in continuing this college experience?* As far as I could tell in those moments, all it ever did was hurt me and spit at my efforts. My friends, my perception of status, and my motivation all stemmed from that relationship.

In high school I had a few solid friends, but I kept my circle small. I was an introvert, but more than that I was an incredibly shy person with interests that I didn't view as "black enough" to share with most of my peers. My biggest secrets being that my favorite band was an alternative rock group called Motion City Soundtrack and I binged anime as if it gave me life. I made friends with a few of the band kids, however, I played no instrument and never quite felt like I belonged. It always felt as if they would be having a better time without me. Due to this, an enormous wall of self-doubt and distrust rose before me, and my own restrictive shell kept me from ever trying to conquer it.

Once I got to college I wanted to break through that shell of mine and have a thriving social life. So, on the very first day, I met up with the girl of my eighteen-year-old dreams. She was a fellow freshman I had met online who happened to sport an afro like myself; her wit and humor both matched the alluring beauty of her light eyes and ecru skin. Her bubbly personality mixed with a sassy attitude enamored everyone around her within a matter of days, turning her into one of the most popular girls I had ever known. I thought if I could somehow make her mine, my life would change in every possible way. Luckily, she had an interest in yours truly.

Low and behold a few weeks later we were officially a couple and my social life seemed to soar beyond anything I could have even dreamed of back in high school. I gained friends and people started inviting me to large get-togethers. Other men began to tell me they were jealous and surprised that someone as quiet as me could get her to be my girlfriend; it was like walking down the red carpet every time someone spotted her on my arm.

Most importantly though, I became motivated. All I ever wanted in life was a loving family to call my own; the classic wife and kids. I didn't enroll in college to obtain knowledge or enter the field of my dreams, but only to get a degree that could help me attain a job I would need to support that family. Family was the only factor in my life that always felt constant as I grew up. No matter where the military sent us, I could always count on them. At some point in time, my life became dedicated to the simple goal of creating a family just as supportive and affectionate as the one that raised me.

Unfortunately, I was also quite lackadaisical when it came to my studies. In high school I never needed to study, and everything came as naturally to me as breathing. Thanks to the many warnings of teachers, I knew college would be more difficult and soon I would be forced to work at my studies in earnest for the first time, but I feared my lack of experience with studying would be my downfall. As luck would have it though, I was able to find a girlfriend early in my college career, and I felt that as long as I kept her happy, the family I sought was within my grasp. I refused to let it slip through my fingers, and thus had found the spark I would need to wholeheartedly put in the work that higher learning expected of me.

Everything was going great for the first two and a half months, and we even got to the point where we said "I love you" to each other. Then her mother came into the picture. Seeing me as nothing more than a distraction, she demanded that her daughter end our relationship and cut all ties with me. In defiance, we continued to date in secret for two months, doing everything a normal couple would do, but hidden from her family. With her mother unaware of our covert romance, everything seemed to be going swimmingly. Then suddenly, with Valentine's Day less than two weeks away, her roommate asked me to stop coming around because my now ex-girlfriend didn't want to see me anymore. Hearing that was like being hit by a train. Not only because I was going to be alone for the day of love, but because I was now going to be alone in my college life.

It quickly became apparent that all of the friends I had made during my first semester in college truly belonged to her. Almost immediately I felt them become cold toward me and I was pushed out of the group. Even the guys on my dorm room floor, who once spoke to me about how jealous they were, had stopped including me in conversations; my status was gone. Possibly worst of all, my newfound motivation for learning was being smothered under the heavy blanket of sorrow. Why continue to work hard when there was no guarantee I would ever find another girl that would date me, much less fall in love with me?

With these thoughts in my mind, I stayed in my room and wept for the days that followed the receipt of that heartbreaking message. Looking back, it was a bit dramatic, but my seemingly certain future of loneliness was all I could think about as tears streamed down my face. It was what I dreamt about when I slept. It was what I repeated to myself in whispers through mouthfuls of chocolate until the box was emptier than my stomach or my heart - emptier than my soul on the third day of this emotional episode.

Hours after I ran out of chocolate, sometime during the ungodly hours of that fateful night, I finally got up for food. I slid my scrawny self out of bed, letting gravity do most of the work; I didn't care if it hurt hitting the floor from the top bunk. I obviously deserved it. After throwing on some random clothes, I walked to the building in the middle of Presidents Park known as Eisenhower. It was where many freshmen hung out during the days and nights at Mason, especially those searching for a quick bite at the only late-night dining option that didn't require a journey across campus, Ike's. But since I wasn't in the mood to be surrounded by a drunk and merry crowd, my destination was the vending machine that stood in the tv room on the opposite side of the building.

The only people awake at that hour were those cramming for exams in the upcoming week and others trying to find their way home after a night of fun I pessimistically believed I would never experience again. I looked at both these kinds of people with the ultimate disdain as I made my way to the hopefully empty tv room. Anger began to fill my heart, though not deservedly so. Finally, I reached the vending machine, thinking about nothing more than how much I hated everything at that moment as I inserted my quarters. Then I heard them. The words that would change the entire trajectory of my life:

"Are you okay?"

Chapter 1

Hinata House

"Are you okay?"

I was shocked by the husky voice that rang out from behind me. I had no idea anyone else was in the room and I was still facing the vending machine, staring straight ahead as I heard my gummy bears fall to the pick-up box below. The idea that a stranger wanted to talk to me, I repeat me, seemed odd. I knew I would never want to talk to *me* about how I was feeling, why would someone else? This simple act of kindness, this inquiry into the soul of a complete stranger, was enough to shatter the bubble of negative emotions I was encased in. My blinders were knocked off and I could begin to truly see my surroundings for what they were.

I spun around and surveyed the room for the owner of that mysterious and caring voice. As I turned, I realized the room was much larger than I allowed myself to notice when I first walked in. The area near the door had a large sectional couch that had seen better days and was fixed in front of a flat screen tv set. The back wall of the room contained large windows with tall desks and chairs lined up next to them. On the far end of the room, the side housing the vending machines, there was a billiards table. As I looked up and across its emerald surface, I noticed there was a man sitting in a tall chair on the other end. Though he was seated, it was easy to discern his towering and well-built figure. He had a low trimmed haircut and a well-kept beard that matched his clean-cut New York style. But one fact surprised me most of all.

Not only did a mystery man ask about my current emotional state, but this man was black. In 2012, a black man talking about his emotions was already quite the rare sight, let alone inquiring about another black man's obvious distress. I would have assumed this was the routine "check" that every black person does to confirm another person isn't dangerous in a questionable environment or situation, but the genuine tone of his voice told me instantly he honestly wanted to know.

Nevertheless, I was going to give my "tough guy" answer; showing weakness was unthinkable. Even if I did want to tell the truth, I was certain no one would be willing to spend the time it would take to listen to the large amount of baggage I was carrying. I opened my mouth, ready to say, "yeah man, I'm okay," and be on my way. Ready to start slinking myself back to my depressing room with my newly acquired treats to feed my sadness. With tears in my eyes, I looked into his and told him "No."

For the rest of the night, we talked -or maybe it would be more accurate to say, I spilled my heart out while he listened. I told him everything that had happened since I arrived at Mason. I told him about my friendships and relationships that had been ending, how I was unsure about my future, and the gnawing loneliness I felt all hours of the day. I couldn't keep anything in anymore and it felt great. Not because I had someone to hear me speak, but because someone was actively listening. He was engaged for the entire conversation. As we wandered around the building with no destination in mind, sharing the chewy, fruit-flavored snacks that wreaked havoc on my braces, he listened. I know this because he asked questions about my situation that no one else had asked me all week. Hell, barring my loving parents, he asked me more questions about my life than anyone had asked me before. However, unlike with my parents, I was willing to answer them openly and honestly.

During our impromptu heart to heart, he never once made me feel crazy. Speaking to him made my head feel so much clearer and my heart so much lighter. While I was far from being over my yet-to-be-acknowledged emotional issues, I could feel that somewhere on the horizon was actual, factual, reachable happiness; that there were people out there with whom I could resonate and form genuine lifelong friendships with. I asked the man his name, and it was laughable. His name was Anthony. We joked that only an Anthony can understand the problems of another Anthony before he recounted some of his own girl troubles and we continued to laugh at each other's misfortunes; deep belly laughs that can only be shared by people wallowing in a similar volume of misery. By the time we realized it, we had been talking for nearly three hours and the sun was about to rise.

At that point, exhaustion began to set in my body. While I had been in my bed all week, I had never truly rested. Our long conversation and the sudden relief of my woes for a couple hours had allowed me to finally notice how dog-tired I was. So, as I began to take my leave, I asked Anthony why he was even awake so late; simply playing pool by himself. He told me that he had severe insomnia and whenever he couldn't sleep he would come down and play pool; hoping that while he improved his game, he would get tired enough to fall asleep. While I felt extremely guilty for leaving him alone and awake after he had helped me, I couldn't help but make the joke that it was probably because his last name was so close to the word lunar; Lunan was meant to be up with the moon. We laughed once more, and I made my leave, hoping and praying I had found a genuine friend. I fell asleep that morning as soon as my head hit my pillow. And, for the first time all week, I rested.

I didn't go to class that day. I just slept. Once I woke up, I embarrassingly went straight to Eisenhower to see if Lunan was still there. He wasn't, so I tried again half an hour later with the same result. I checked three times more after that in quick succession until I finally convinced myself to stop. During each search I felt silly, but I couldn't help but chase that dragon of wholesome, brotherly connection. Once I gave up, I went about my day as normal; staring at my phone, hoping for a text - whenever I wasn't journeying across mystical lands in search of grey-bearded monks and ancient dragons to slay on my tiny dinosaur tv and XBOX 360 that I had brought with me to college. After the sun had set, I grabbed some dinner from the Johnson Center on campus and I decided to stop by Eisenhower one more time before I went to bed. Thanks to most classes being finished for the day, the tv room was now packed with students gathering around the television and studying at the high tables along the window. I grew nervous amongst the small crowd as I tried to avoid any conversation or eye contact while I scanned the room, but it didn't take long for me to see a tall and familiar figure by the pool table. Lunan was playing with some friends, though for the life of me I can't remember who. Regardless, I didn't feel welcome.

It wasn't a difficult task, convincing myself I wasn't. I was already apprehensive about making friends and had no interest in forming connections that wouldn't stand the test of time. The effort it took to overcome my shy nature was too much to waste on relationships that would probably fall apart within months; the mental exhaustion caused by navigating small talk and avoiding embarrassment gave me headaches and was something I dreaded and avoided at all costs. Furthermore, I didn't think Lunan would want the sad guy from the night before to hang out with his real friends. This feeling had less to do with them, and more to do with my own perception of how much people enjoyed my presence. Then, noticing me near the entrance, Lunan surprised me once again by waving me over to play without saying a word and brandishing a shining smile.

From then on we hung out quite a bit and typically we could be found playing pool in that same room. Through our countless games, I couldn't help but watch how social Lunan truly was. He'd invite anyone who entered the room to play; regardless of if he knew them or whether or not they were alone. Even if they said no, it wouldn't be a surprise to see Lunan carry on a pleasant conversation with them during our game. This amazed me to no end and struck me as more of an innate talent than a mere personality trait. Interactions as simple as asking for directions or speaking to a cute girl that happened to be my lab partner made my heartbeat fast and heavy. Even speaking to friends of friends caused me to feel awkward and shrink. I would hesitate to even smile back at a pretty cashier; fearing my smile was ungainly. In contrast to Lunan, I was a bonafide mess.

After about a week filled with an innumerable amount of billiard matches, we grew bored of the routine and Lunan introduced me to a wonderful game that would provide me with the opportunity to speak to new people one on one. The paragon of accessible strategy games: chess. The day Lunan taught me this mental sport, I also met another man who would change my life and continue to inspire me every day: Charles Stewart.

Charles had walked into the common area of Lunan's dorm building with a group of friends while Lunan and I were engaged in a teaching game. Ever an amiable man, and in typical Lunan fashion, he invited them over to play a couple games with us. They declined of course; I was still learning to play, and most people would rather not spend a weekend night playing chess. Sheepish as ever, I was happy with the answer. As embarrassing as it is to say, the thought of playing chess in front of the cute girls in Charles' group made me nervous. Especially one in particular. Beyond being a beautiful Latina, her cool and irreverent demeanor triggered something in me. She was the first girl that made my heart race since my breakup, and I hadn't even met her yet; nor was I ready to. So unsurprisingly, I let out a sigh of relief as Lunan and I continued our game and our conversation with the group ended, though every now and again I peeked over Lunan's shoulder to sneak a glance at the spellbinding beauty in the jean jacket.

Days later I would finally get my chance to properly meet Charles. Charles had made his way to the room in Eisenhower where we always spent our free time and took up Anthony's offer to play a few rounds. During our game, we spoke only about the basic "get to know you" rhetoric that was common in college. Where are you from? What's your major? Etcetera. But as mundane as the conversation seemed, this was an intense victory. The chess match on the board was a perfect metaphor for how I felt on the inside. I was new at this, I wasn't as good as my opponent, and the whole situation felt as intense as staring down a wild bear in the woods. Yet, this in and of itself was a victory for me. I was speaking to a stranger normally, and, despite the intensity I felt, I was enjoying it! I began to think, *Maybe I can do this. Maybe I can finally break through this seemingly impregnable shell of mine.*

Charles can be summarized in a single phrase: Thought-provoking. I would come to learn this as the days passed and we played more games. With him around, every day seemed to bring with it a new lesson or philosophical question begging to be pondered. No matter the topic, Charles could flip it upside down and shake something out that could rattle the foundation of your beliefs. Anything, from the complex concepts of politics and religion to the purportedly simple idea of what a conversation is, was liable to be dissected and studied.

Over the next couple of weeks, I met several more lovable and quirky characters via our shared friendship with Lunan. We became our own little Eisenhower Crew and eventually became so interconnected that we didn't need to have Lunan present to enjoy each other's company. There was John, the highly intelligent but slothful man hailing from Woodbridge, Virginia, and Ayush, his more driven and energetic best friend. There was also Nicole. She was a very quiet, serious, and oftentimes mean-spirited girl; she was affectionate in her own way, though from outside the group it may have been impossible to discern. I had a slight crush on her when I had first met her as well, though this dissipated quickly as we became friends. Next, there was the joker of our group, Moses. He didn't go to Mason, but often came to visit the campus and hang out in Eisenhower. While Moses was funny, his actions were more so. His ability to convince any individual wandering through Eisenhower to buy him full meals at Ike's rivaled Lunan's ability to hold up a conversation with anybody. We would watch in awe as he spoke to total strangers and walked away with burgers, fries, drinks, and cookies. While his methods were lucid, using them proved unsuccessful for anyone but Moses. Must have been the charm.

Every day at least a few of us would get together and relax in the same tv room where I had met Lunan; playing our typical games of chess and billiards, or having deep conversations that opened our minds to new ideas. Many days we would just ride along with Lunan as he suffered from a particularly bad episode of insomnia, watching classic late-night television like Assy McGee.

No matter how stressed I was by the events of that semester, that place became my safe haven. It was my Hinata House. A place where people from different backgrounds can come together, experience companionship, and learn from one another. And much like the manga Love-Hina, the story in which the aforementioned house takes place, we would all come to grow from our shared experiences.

Chapter 2

Anthony No Basket

Thanks to the Eisenhower Crew, my conversational prowess improved dramatically within a matter of weeks. Lunan roped me into many-a- conversation I would have avoided otherwise, boosting my tolerance with speaking to strangers.

Charles, being ever sagacious, constantly caused passionate group debates to ignite with his philosophical and rhetorical questions. Though these often left me feeling frustrated to the point where I could feel the veins on my forehead pulsating, I became more comfortable with voicing my opinions. At least when it came to our crew.

Nicole, thanks to her often sardonic attitude, helped me feel more comfortable around women and gave me a thicker skin. If there was something to criticize you about, she would let you know without restraint.

Lastly, John, Ayush, and Moses would reliably supply us with so much silly and random conversation that the idea of talking about any given topic on my mind became less scary.

A couple of weeks after I had met Charles; he, Lunan, and I started going to SouthSide together at least once per day. This was where we would often meet in order to not only take advantage of Lunan's unlimited entry swipes into the dining hall, but to hang out and just be guys. Since they could tell I was growing more confident, we started a new after meal tradition: challenging one another to flirt with random girls that happened to be sitting near our table, using some ridiculous one liner we had devised as a group. Despite my progress, I didn't have the courage of our resident social savant, so I would punk out every time. Charles would follow my example in most cases as well, due to the absurdity of the scripts we had crafted, but Lunan...well he was certainly made different from the rest of us. Any pick-up line, any girl, any time. No condition we concocted could dissuade him. Lunan was not only the social king of our group, but he was the bonafide master of coquetry as well. I equally admired and envied his ability to risk rejection with such an unflappable confidence.

During one of our lunches in SouthSide, probably while the three of us were discussing the next dare, something near the entrance caught my eye. It was a big poofy afro standing above the crowd, waiting in line to get inside. I stared as the large puff of hair bounced with each step forward; missing my own afro that I had chopped off only a few days earlier. I told myself at the time I had to cut it off to get a decent job, but deep down even I knew the truth. It was a physical manifestation of my emotional attempt to cut off the past. A removal of my old ways, and the representation of my hope to mature into something better. So, while I admired what I saw and began to regret my decision, it dawned on me that afros weren't the most common sight on campus. I stared at the line intently; knowing there were only a handful of people it could belong to and praying my suspicions about the identity of the owner were wrong. As they stepped to the front of the line, I winced; recognizing who it was the instant their face became visible. There she was, my ex, whom I hadn't seen or spoken to since she broke up with me out of the blue via her roommate - Amber.

She noticed me almost immediately and her mouth dropped to the floor. I half expected a look of disgust to come afterward, but to my surprise she giggled and turned to her friends. They all looked, smiled, and continued to laugh amongst themselves as they walked past our table.

Lunan tried to convince me that I should try to go talk to her, but I refused outright; explaining that she wasn't smiling at me. She was simply entertained by the idea that I had cut my hair after a breakup like a distraught schoolgirl. To me, there was no other explanation. The subject was dropped, and we finished our food.

While leaving, Lunan asked if we wanted to play basketball at the gym in the adjacent building. Charles had other plans for the afternoon, so he declined. I, on the other hand, had nothing to do and I wasn't in the mood to be alone. Still, basketball was the last thing on earth I wanted to do, so sitting alone in my room seemed like the better option in comparison. Lunan had asked me to play several times since we had met, but I turned him down on each occasion. I hated the sport. The mere proposal to play filled me with nothing but insecurities and anxiety. I rejected the game so fervently each time he urged me to join him, that it would leave any witness wondering what was wrong with me - and something was. But to be honest, at that point in my life I couldn't recall what it was. I had pushed the reasoning to the recesses of my mind long ago.

Yet, in spite of my reservations, I finally conceded to Lunan. *I'm already working hard to conquer my shyness, so why not tackle this?* I thought. I wasn't wearing the proper attire, so I ran to my dorm to get ready and quickly dashed back to the gym across from SouthSide. By the time I returned, Lunan had signed out one of the basketballs and was chatting up the attendant at the front desk. We turned to enter the courts that were situated behind towering windows and a glass door, and then suddenly, a strange feeling erupted within me. I began to shake and perspire. An irrepressible compulsion to run arose from what seemed like my very soul. Through grit alone, I fought my instincts and followed Lunan through the door and onto the courts. This feeling wasn't normal, and I wanted to get over it; I had no choice but to face my fears.

Upon walking through what felt like the gates of Hades, we noticed an open net on the far end of the court. Lunan dribbled the ball as we moseyed over, brimming with excitement. Suddenly, like a strike of lightning, he tossed me the ball and told me to take the first shot. The ball hit my chest before being ensnared in my arms - which had jolted up out of shock to catch it. Seeing the ball nestled in my trembling arms unlocked something I had repressed long ago. I remembered everything. My current pathetic state was all thanks to the most humiliating moment of my young life. An event that took place during my middle school years.

***

Eighth grade. That time of puberty and social risk and reward everyone looks back on fondly. It probably isn't shocking that I was far shyer during this period, than I was at nineteen years old. Yet, by some odd stroke of luck, I had made quite a few friends. My friends were on sports teams, ace students, and considered to be the most popular among all the students in the entire school. They were all but famous amongst us kids, while I was merely cool adjacent.

I'm certain our friendships only started as a result of the close proximity of our homes, and the fact that my grades placed me in the same honors classes as them. We were all military brats, and we all lived on Fort Drum. Fort Drum was the largest military base I had ever lived on, and it was located in upstate New York. Forest separated the many family-filled neighborhoods from not only each other, but most military activities on base. So much forest in fact, that we normally forwent the sidewalks and travelled through those so called "woods" to reach each other's houses. Oftentimes we would spend hours in these forests, and our adventures took us all over the base where fences didn't prevent us from going further. Getting lost in those ever-expanding woods was a dream, and I loved every moment spent in them.

The only outdoor activity that could get me out of those woods was, naturally, basketball. And I was damn good. I could keep up with any of my pals on the basketball team shot for shot. Every one-on-one game was fierce, and while I didn't always win, I never made it easy. I was often asked to try out for our middle school's team, but I was much too bashful for the idea to be more than a passing thought. So, I chose to simply revel in any victory I had against my friends who had joined the team themselves. This way I could prove to myself how good I was, without the judgment that I associated with team sports. However, eventually this became unsatisfying. Fortunately, a special event would give me the opportunity to shoot for greater heights.

Within our circle, there was a competition more important than any school sponsored match. It was a little basketball tournament held on Fort Drum called Midnight Basketball. It took place once a month, and as the name implies, it was held late in the night. The teams played games of three versus three with one substitute on the bench. The prizes for victory were t-shirts featuring the event's logo and bragging rights for the coming month.

As I continued to gain prowess in the sport, I fantasized about winning this tournament and spearheading my team to victory. Sadly, my hopes of ever competing in this tournament were imprisoned behind the steel bars of my shy demeanor; hidden in the shadows of my fear of failing in front of others. My best excuse for never trying to break out of this jail was that my friends' team already had a full roster of four that they played with every month, and I took solace in this. It meant I could continue to dream comfortably while telling myself it was impossible to achieve.

Then, the impossible happened; a spot opened up. One of my friends was going to be out of town during the upcoming tournament, and I was the team's first choice to substitute him.

They were the best possible Midnight Basketball team that one could wish to join; all the members were on our middle school basketball team. Better yet, this was a team that had won second place almost every time. A team that had only ever lost to one other; a team that was made up of high schoolers - two of which happened to be older brothers to two of the members of my friends' team. Time and time again I would hear about how this team of middle schoolers had come oh-so close to winning Midnight Basketball. This was my chance to lift this team up. A team that had smelled the spoils of victory but never tasted it, while watching the joy it put on their brother's faces. This was my opportunity to be the hero that finally helped their team champion over this perceived Goliath. I could already hear the cheers of the crowd for my great triumph.

So, I agreed to participate in the tournament and began training harder than ever before. I played against anyone I could in the neighborhood; I even played games of two versus one. I wanted to make sure I'd be ready for this once in a lifetime opportunity. Failure was not an option. The night of the game, I felt beyond ready and bathed in the warmth of knowing that soon I would be one of the popular kids myself. No longer would I be just the silent friend who barely spoke.

Once the first round started, I quickly got on my guy and started playing defense. I'd been training for weeks; I was sure there was no way he could get past me. Then he did something I wasn't ready for; something I never pictured in my wildest fantasies.

He passed the ball.

Time began to move slowly as I watched the ball zip past me, and I realized that I had no idea how to play on a team. I had no sense of awareness on a court; I didn't know where my teammates were, let alone the members of the opposing team. All those games of two vs one meant nothing because I played them against younger kids in the neighborhood.

As the ball reached my opponent's teammate, it finally dawned on me that my thoughts of being the key to my team's victory were nothing more than delusions of grandeur. The noise of the crowd was muted by the cry of a voice in my head, **"you will fail."**

And fail I did. The game continued to go downhill faster and faster as it progressed. I wasn't passing the ball correctly, I often had the ball stolen from me, and I could never cover my guy properly. I had lost all composure. Each failure made the voice echo louder; **"You will fail!"** After the opposing team racked up enough points to almost warrant a mercy rule within a matter of minutes, I was benched. This should have been a relief, but it only served to change the voice to a somber and disheartening **"You failed."**

I'd like to say that our team made a comeback, but the damage was done. We lost the game, and I had brought this second-place team all the way down to the bottom. *Losing in the first round? How did that happen?* I wondered as my body shook from the embarrassment.

While my friends were not unkind to me after the loss, I felt nothing but shame. I sat on the bench wide-eyed and fighting back tears, gripping my thighs so tightly that my nails nearly broke the skin, and lamenting the lost respect of my teammates.

I had failed in front of everyone I knew in middle school, including my crush who was in the crowd watching the game. I decided to hide myself near the snack table close to the bathroom until it was time for my parents to pick me up; only moving away from my hiding spot occasionally to avoid having "weirdo" added to my new "loser" descriptor. Everything that happened that night justified what I had always thought before. I had never felt such emotional distress when I stayed in my safe shell, so I dove right back in, fortified it, and padded it with a new disdain for the game of basketball. From that day on, unless it was with my baby brother or required by gym class, I never played the sport of basketball again.

***

The stroll down Trauma Lane had come and gone in a flash. Now I understood why I was standing there nervously with a ball in my arms; my heart pounding against it through my chest. Every pleasant memory I had of the game was all but erased by my middle school failure, and to make matters worse I was hyper aware of the difference in skill between a quitter like me and other young black men on the court who had been playing most of their lives. Exposing myself to the opportunity of experiencing public ridicule once again felt insane.

But instead of passing the ball back to Lunan and turning tail, I took the first shot and a game of HORSE commenced. I loathed the idea of playing ball, but it would have been mortifying to have Lunan see me as a coward. While it may not have been a true game of basketball, this was yet another stepping-stone for me.

At the end of the game, a group of guys approached us and asked if we wanted to play a round of three versus three. "Nope." - That would have been my immediate response if I wasn't left tongue-tied by a mental rollercoaster of anxiety and fear. Lunan answered before I could even form a complete thought, and to no one's surprise, he accepted the offer.

As I began to feel doomed within my situation, something beautiful came to everyone's attention. God must have been showing me pity, because low and behold there were one too many people for the game. Out of character, I burst into the discussion and hastily volunteered to sit out. Though everyone was perplexed by my sudden resignation, they accepted my proposal and divided themselves up into teams. I doubt I could have appeared more eager to be uninvolved as I skipped to the sidelines. I gleefully pulled out my phone and sat, not once looking at the game in front of me.

My mind wandered as I scrolled aimlessly. The events of the day playing through my mind like some mundane highlight reel. That's when my mind recalled lunch and seeing my ex-girlfriend. After that, she was all I could think about as Lunan's comment about speaking to her reverberated in my head. Part of me wanted to know why she had cut ties with me to begin with, and the other part just wanted to see her smile again.

Since I was riding high off my personal victory of making it onto the court, I convinced myself without much difficulty that she'd love to see how much I had changed since we had gone our separate ways. I decided to send her a text, and then I texted her friend for good measure. To my surprise they both responded quickly and seemed happy to hear from me.

By the time Lunan had finished his game, I had somehow arranged a double date between the four of us. While I knew that being romantic again wasn't in the cards, some part of me still wanted to be friends with my ex. In my mind, she was the most important part of my college experience thus far. And it went without saying that I still missed her.

I was so giddy about the date, that when the day arrived I couldn't help but prepare myself hours in advance. While it wasn't a real date per se, I would get to see her again and that was all I cared about.

Lunan had his reservations, seeing I may have been too excited, but he was happy for me. I was dressed in the most stylish outfit I could put together. You know the deal, even if she didn't want me back romantically, I had to show her what she was missing. And hey, a boy can hope right?

As we approached the restaurant known as Pilot House, I could see Amber through the window talking to her friend. They were smiling and laughing without a care in the world. At that moment, I wanted her back more than anything. I was so excited; it took everything I had not to run into the arms of the girl that had been the object of my infatuation. Once we entered the dining hall and approached the table, I greeted them with the biggest smile the muscles in my face could muster. Instantly, Amber's face turned grim in response. While her friend welcomed us with a warm grin and hello, Amber was cold and crossed her arms, seemingly in protest of the entire situation at hand. A single reluctant "Hi" came from her lips. I became downcast as I realized that she did not want to be there, and that it was her friend that must have convinced her to give me a chance. The illusion was broken, and it was clear that the night wasn't going to be enjoyable.

For the rest of the night, Lunan and her friend did most of the talking. If I had to take a shot in the dark, I would say Amber spoke to me directly ten times the entire hour we were there.

On the walk home, I was crestfallen and couldn't help but think of how idiotic I had been, thinking that she wanted to see me in the first place. Back in Eisenhower, Lunan tried to convince me that it would simply take time for her to open back up. I wanted to believe him more than anything, even while staring at evidence to the contrary. On my phone was a recent tweet from the very woman we were talking about, and she was clearly quite displeased by that little outing. While I can't remember the post verbatim, it could be summed up with, "You can't come back into my life after leaving for over a month."

Reading her true thoughts left me further devastated, but more than that it left me befuddled. She had broken up with me and it was never my choice to exit her life. I leered at my phone screen, refusing to acknowledge that all hope was lost despite the proof in front of my eyes. In the end, through the combined forces of cognitive dissonance and the hope in Lunan's words, I convinced myself I just needed to be more present in her life and prove I could be a great friend. I was certain she would eventually see my efforts and welcome me back with open arms. But naturally, my unwelcomed olive branches would only make things worse.

For a brief time, I continued to text her thinking my attempts to rebuild our connection couldn't possibly go unrewarded. She seemed friendly in the messages, but sadly the more I tried, the worse she spoke of me to friends and the worse her posts became online. While she never used my name, the posts were clearly about me due to the details mentioned within them. After a couple weeks, I finally gave up. Even Lunan with his ever-positive attitude was eventually forced to admit the situation seemed hopeless.

I felt embarrassed. I realized that my efforts at keeping her in my life were just coming off as clingy. I was a fool pining for the attention of someone who no longer cared for him. Clearly she had moved on; she had joined a new church group, her social life boomed without me around to hold her back, and through the grapevine I heard she had even found a new love interest that happened to look like an older version of me. I was wasting my time.

So, I decided to end it permanently, sending her a text one last time in order to let her know that she would no longer be hearing from me; as soon as she returned my favorite pajama pants, that is. While we were dating in secret, I had lent them to her on a freezing winter night after we had left a party on campus. All she had to protect her from the cold wind was a thin purple dress, and, since my dorm was close by, stopping to pick up some pants for her felt like the gentlemanly thing to do.

While I truly wanted my pants back, there was more to it than just regaining my most comfortable sleepwear. One last meeting would give me the opportunity to get everything off my chest. To let her know how upset I was about what had been going on the past couple of weeks. I realized I had become a huge pest for her, but I wished she had been more upfront with me, rather than speak badly about me behind my back on social media.

Though she was cordial, it was obvious that she was reluctant to see me once more. Still, she agreed and that same afternoon I made my way to her dorm with Lunan in tow. While my confidence had grown, I needed someone there to make sure that I didn't fold before I even reached her building. He was less my backup in a potentially heated conversation, and more of a sponsor helping me stay committed to the progress I was making in rehab.

During the walk to the dorm, we talked about everything that had transpired over the course of my brief relationship with Amber. How Amber and I probably got together too soon after meeting each other. How it wasn't anybody's fault that it didn't work out, but it was merely a difference in personalities, upbringings, and hobbies, and nothing more. While I thought I had found someone in her that I loved, in reality I had just clung to the first girl that showed an interest in me; not caring if we were compatible or not. As my journey across campus with Lunan continued, I could feel any anger I had toward her begin to dissipate.

As we approached her building, Amber told us she was already on her way down. Despite being at peace with what was happening, I was still nervous about expressing my feelings. Thank God Lunan was there, or I probably would have turned tail and ran as I predicted. Peering through the glass doors, I could see her exit the elevator. She seemed irritated once again, but not furious. I became focused on my goal, and mentally prepared myself for the fiery ending to this freshman year fling.

She opened the door with one hand; leaning out without stepping a single foot outside the threshold of the door. I didn't bother reaching out to take the door from her as I had no intention of entering. Tension was in the air. Our eyes were locked, waiting for the other to say something inflammatory that would turn this into an impassioned quarrel. Then, without either party saying "hi", I asked her if she had the pants. She held them out to me through the crack of the door and gave me a simple, "here you go." What happened next still amazes me to this day:

I took the pants and we said bye.

That was it. No argument. No insults. Zero passions and emotions were exchanged. The tumultuous relationship that laid the framework for my freshmen year ended calmer than I could have ever foretold. I guess at some point during our trek to Amber's dorm, Lunan made me realize that airing my grievances would be pointless. It didn't matter why she broke up with me and it didn't matter why she chose to belittle and disparage me online instead of talking to me directly. Our breakup was inevitable, so knowing the truth wouldn't change a thing. It was best to leave it in the past and focus on my future.

With the pajamas back in my hands, we commenced our hike back to Presidents Park to meet up with the rest of our crew, anticipating another night of fiery debates and games of chess.

Chapter 3

A Night Out

"You need to get a haircut." Nicole asserted frankly
and in her notoriously monotone voice. It had been over a
month since I had my afro cut off, and my hair was starting to
get wild in spite of my regular use of a durag to keep it under
control. The once smooth waves that had been produced by
my new habit of constantly brushing my hair and wearing the
silky black headwrap were now looking more akin to choppy
waters during a storm at sea.

"I should have known better than to ask you." I said
feeling a twitch in my right eye. "If I knew a black barber
around here that wasn't a billion miles away, I'd have gotten
that done already." When I got my afro chopped off, I was
visiting one of my friends back in Portsmouth, Virginia; a
town three hours away from Mason where I had spent most of
my high school years. I had gone to the neighborhood
barbershop I used to visit every two weeks for a shape-up,

and my usual barber, who went by the moniker of Q, had the honors of carrying out my afro's execution.

"You could always try the shop in my neighborhood. It's only about half an hour away, so I could give you a ride the next time I drive down to visit my parents." Charles offered kindly.

I turned down the offer, thinking that since the semester was going to be over within a matter of weeks, I might as well wait until I was back home and my father could handle the haircut himself. Besides, I was only concerned about my appearance because that night, unlike every other one that semester, Lunan and I were going to be spending our night away from Eisenhower's common room.

You would think the combined forces of college freedom and an emotionally liberating moment would lead to an exciting new chapter in my life, but no. By and large, many would consider what followed quite boring. My life was basically the same as it had been before my failed effort to bring Amber back into my life. The only true change we had made to our daily activities came via Charles.

Charles had mentioned off-hand that dragging himself to the gym regularly was becoming difficult, and that maybe if he had a partner he would go more frequently. Since I had been putting off my goal to hit the gym and put some meat on my bones, this seemed like a grand opportunity. Charles was on the track team back in high school, and had a slim, athletic build that I secretly envied. So, I offered to be his new partner, thinking he seemed as qualified as anyone to help me exercise properly. But besides that small inclusion, I was content with the routine days and nights I had with the Eisenhower Crew, so efforts to alter them were far and few between.

"You ready, Ant?" Lunan questioned after checking the time. "It's about time we headed over."

I rolled my eyes and groaned. "Yeah, let's go," I bemoaned as I stood up and followed him out the door. Being torn out of my literal comfort zone for what would be an extended period of time was annoying, but I knew this was a necessary evil. That night we were going to get to know our future roommates: Xavier and Nick.

Back in late February, Lunan had jumped at the chance when I suggested we should be roommates during our sophomore year, even though we had only known each other for a couple of weeks. Unfortunately, we had no other friends to add to our group since the other members of the Eisenhower Crew had already selected their future roommates by the time I had met them. With the housing application deadline fast approaching, we were left with no choice but to turn to the internet where there was an online group for GMU students desperately searching for roommates for the upcoming semester. Through this, we connected with Xavier and Nick, who also needed two more people to fill out their roster.

In spite of the due date for the application growing ever closer, we thought it was still prudent that we met up with Xavier in Southside in order to get a feel for whether or not we would all be a good fit together. Xavier was a soft-spoken young black man that was slightly shorter than me, but stood tall with his cool and confident demeanor.

Valedictorian of his graduating class; he was smart to boot. On the surface, we had plenty in common, and we liked him well enough. Nick, on the other hand, was a complete mystery to us since he wasn't able to meet us for the dinner. Xavier had only described him as a very chill and laid-back dude who loved to party on the weekends; a pretty generic description that left much to the imagination.

"I hope Nick is as cool as Xavier." Lunan mused as we headed toward their building with a tepid May wind at our backs.

"Same, even though it's too late to care now." I pointed out with a chuckle. We had signed the housing applications months ago based purely on the good vibrations of Xavier alone, thinking anyone he chose to associate with couldn't have been a bad person. "If he's as cool as Xavier says, maybe he'll be able to help us finally get into a party." I added with a pained grin, remembering the sole night I had chosen to diverge from most of our group in pursuit of something more.

***

It was a single event that tempted me to veer toward the wild side; the release of a certain movie at the campus theater: Project X. I had gone to see the film with the Eisenhower Crew and boy, did that movie blow me away. A movie filled with such intense partying and euphoria that I wanted to rush out of the theater mid-film and go on a bender that would last until sunrise. Once the movie ended, I began contacting everyone I knew on campus to find a party while adrenaline pumped through my veins.

Since I didn't know anyone in a fraternity, my options were limited to the few classmates I had mustered up the courage to speak with and the floormates I still spoke to; neither of whom were too keen on replying to me. I couldn't blame them though, it was my own fault for having rejected every one of my floormates' invitations in the past, and no one wants the nervous guy from BIO 210 randomly asking them for addresses to parties. Everyone else in our crew, whose hunger for a night out nearly rivaled my own, joined in the search after my swift failure, each one sending out messages to whoever they knew like cursed chain-letters. It wasn't until at least an hour had passed, and our butts were firmly planted on the couch in Eisenhower, that we finally obtained a building and room number for a campus dorm party. However, the search had taken so long that the enthusiasm of Nicole, Lunan, and Charles had died. After some deliberation within the group, only John and I ended up at the door of the party; our thirsts needed to be satiated.

I knocked on the door nervously while John stood behind me in anticipation. The door swung open abruptly and we were hit with a wave of heat and the stench of sweat-drenched bodies. As far as the eye could see, young adults were huddled together like penguins sitting on eggs. Instinctively, I turned around, passed John, and left without saying a word to whomever opened the door. *The rest of the Eisenhower Crew was right not to come.* I judged. John was hesitant to follow, but after looking back at the party and being faced with the unwelcoming gaze of the host still holding the door open, he followed suit.

My attempt at creating an exciting party experience had failed, and I never tried again during the few remaining weeks of my freshmen year. Partly because I wanted to avoid another failure, but mostly because the majority of our group, like myself, was introverted by nature. While none of the other crew members were shy like me, they seemed to prefer staying low-key and easygoing. It seemed like we needed nothing more than to hang out with each other while Adult Swim played in the background during our discussions about both the silly and serious; through which slowly but surely these wacky individuals overcame the wall that protected my ego, and I grew closer to them with each passing day.

During my high school years, I felt all but ostracized by the black community at my school. They didn't hate me, but most never found me interesting enough to hold a second conversation. They just couldn't seem to relate to a black kid that enjoyed anime and couldn't name more than five rappers without pausing. One whose fashion tastes veered more toward pop-punk than hip-hop. Even when I was a kid, I was often referred to as a white boy trapped in a black-boy's body by my own family members. While this experience was not unique, anyone who has experienced it can tell you it affects your relationship with the community you were born into. In my case, I became uncomfortable around people with the same skin color as myself, and thus most of my friends throughout high school were white, with the occasional fellow Oreo sprinkled in.

My relationship with my new black friends had been everything I had ever wanted. They never made me feel like I had to "act" Black. I could be myself and show every nerdy side of me. Even if I brought up a topic that wasn't interesting to them, I was never shamed for it. I finally felt like I belonged with my kin, and I was happy to waste my nights away with them.

***

Xavier lived in the same building as Amber and for a moment I was nervous that I would run into her, fearing that she would think I was stalking her. Of course, being spotted was unlikely due to the size of the building, and as Xavier led us to his dorm room it became obvious he even lived on the opposite side from her. My worry was for naught, and I was relieved.

Upon entering their suite, it was impossible not to be enamored by how different it was from the dorms in Presidents Park. They had their own kitchen, living room, and bathrooms, whereas the bathrooms, showers, and common areas we had in Presidents Park were communal. The space was so large we almost hadn't noticed Nick who was situated on the couch with his girlfriend, lying down under a blanket. Upon noticing our presence, he quickly rose to greet us, revealing a frame as scrawny as my own that was engulfed by his baggy shirt with fraternity letters sewn onto the front. Nick had pale white skin and blonde surfer-esque hair that he had to repeatedly flip out of his face as he spoke. He was louder yet somehow more relaxed than Xavier at the same time. He seemed both preppy and down to earth; he exuded levels of nonchalant and confidence that seemed stereotypical of a young white man that had recently been initiated into a fraternity. He reminded me of the same kind of people that I used to find annoying in high school. Funny enough, he was from Virginia Beach, which is only a hop and a skip from my adopted hometown, Portsmouth. While I didn't make a strong connection with Nick that night, I was glad we at least had that in common.

Once we had all gotten settled in their living room, Nick, rubbing his hands while looking around at all of us gleefully, declared "So I think it's time for the main event!"

A half smile crossed my face as I turned and nodded to Lunan. It was story time. Near the end our initial meeting in SouthSide, we learned that Xavier also had a terrible first relationship in college that left him ashamed and confused. He swore it was so dreadful that it could top mine, and of course I disagreed vehemently.

Nick and Lunan both hyped up the sitcom worthiness of our relationships and the breakups that followed as if they had money on which was worse. They had spoken so highly of our stories as we sat in a circle that I feared my tale wouldn't satisfy my now expectant crowd. Yet something about the situation awakened the bard within me, and I began to tell my story with all of the bombast it deserved.

Xavier quickly joined in, and we began spinning a wonderful tandem yarn filled with humor and twists. We joked about our own naivety and foolishness. We made light of all the moments we had made mistakes with our exes. Through it all, we laughed to the point of tears. Thus, was marked the beginning of a beautiful new brotherhood.

While I will not share his story here, as that is his story to tell, I will say he won. I may have been voted Best Storyteller by everyone in the room, but the ending to Xavier's tragedy was too dramatic for me to compete with. My foolish attempts to win Amber back could not compare.

The night ended up being more enjoyable than I predicted. We watched movies, ate pizza, and even shared music playlists. I was happy we made the effort to come and get to know our future suitemates. But all good things must come to an end, and as we started inching toward the door to leave, Xavier spotted that I was losing control of my hair. "You know I can take care of that for you next semester." Xavier offered matter-of-factly. He revealed that he taught himself to cut his own hair before coming to Mason, and he was willing to be our on-campus barber for free; if we liked what we saw that is. "Maybe we can do a test run before I head home for the summer." Xavier added, mentally leafing through his calendar.

Lunan and I looked at each other ecstatically. A trusted black barber was a hard thing to find in Fairfax, Virginia when you didn't have a car. Having one living with you would be a dream.

As far as I was concerned, I had hit the roommate lottery. I was gaining an inside man for frat parties, a barber to keep me looking fresh, and I'd be living with the man that had helped me to course-correct my depressing second semester. The stage was set for a perfect sophomore year.

Chapter 4

End of a Prologue

Before I knew it, summer had come and gone, and I was riding in the back seat of my dad's car as we drove back to Mason. My vacation was rather uneventful since we moved to the boonies of South Carolina the day after my high school graduation the year before, and I was unable to make a single friend in town before leaving for college. While I was short on plans during the break, spending time with my family was a relaxing and welcomed reprise from the stress of academia. It gave me a socially acceptable reason to be a recluse and dive back into my nerdier hobbies. I didn't have to worry about relationships, classes, or making new friends, and while part of me was jealous of some of the fantastical summers I saw my peers enjoying online, I took solace in the thought that I could have all the adventure I wanted when I returned to college. But as the summer came to a close, reality began to set in, and all I could do on that nine-hour drive back to campus was worry.

I was terrified that the distance and time during the summer would have caused our little Eisenhower Crew to grow apart. We had come together in less than three months, so it wasn't impossible for us to fall apart in the same amount of time. Especially when we had lost what connected us to begin with. No longer could I simply walk to the Eisenhower building in the center of Presidents Park, knowing someone would be there waiting to hangout and start a game of pool. We all lived in different areas on campus now, so even if we were still good friends when we got back to George Mason, who was to say it would last? What if we were only friends out of convenience?

I was concerned about dating too. Amber had shared some tweets over the summer that weren't exactly flattering. She was cautioning freshmen women to beware of getting attached to the first man they met in college, using her past relationship with the clingy and undriven loser as an example. While she once again did not name names, everyone in her circle at the time knew I was the infamous boyfriend she spoke of. I became anxious about the idea of walking onto that campus and being rejected by every girl I met. All on the basis of a rumor. Over the summer I continued the workouts I had started with Charles and gained about 30lbs. I was feeling confident with my body for the first time in my life and I was ready to show off my gains. The thought of possibly being rejected due to hearsay after all of my hard work was tremendously discouraging.

All of this coupled, with the fact that I would be living with new people, made me panic internally. Xavier and Nick seemed like amazing people, but I had never thought of myself as very likeable. I was still a timid and awkward kid on the inside, and many people perceived my resulting silence as the sign of a stuck up and self-absorbed personality. I was worried I would waste the good impression Lunan and I had made at the end of our freshmen year, and it made me sick to my stomach. I imagined different scenarios, trying to picture a way to make the perfect impression on my first day as a roommate. I was so fixated I barely realized we had arrived on campus and my father had already parked the car. Trying to calm myself down as I stepped out of the vehicle, I kept telling myself to just be like Lunan. *Just be like Lunan. If you can just do that, there will be no reason to worry about...*

"Hey!!!!"

The loud cry had ripped me out of my own head. I looked around and saw a young black man with two bags and a big suitcase waving his arms wildly like a pool noodle from across the parking garage with a huge grin on his face. It was Xavier. I was embarrassed at the large effort to get my attention, but at the same time I was relieved. Even the best of friends I had within the Eisenhower Crew had never greeted me with such joy. His greeting alone calmed the storm raging in my head. So, I waved back, trying to match his enthusiasm with a shining, tooth-filled smile of my own.

Xavier had arrived on campus about twenty minutes before us and was happy to show the way to the dorm. My parents loved Xavier and his respectful, kind demeanor from the moment they met him. They could tell at first glance he would be a great friend to keep around.

Our dorm was tucked into the corner of the second floor of our building; located right next to the back entrance. The windows overlooked the mini convenience store on the ground floor below, and we had full view of the sidewalk that led to Southside and the center of campus. The suite itself was divided into two halves, each with their own entrance but connected by a bathroom in the middle. Xavier and Nick had their names posted on one of the doors, and on the other was a sign marked with Lunan's and my own. Neither Nick nor Lunan were present when we entered the room, so we just dropped off all of my things and got to know Xavier a bit better as he continued to help us drag everything inside. Once all the bags were hauled into the dorm, Xavier excused himself in order to go meet up with some friends that had just returned to campus. Before leaving though, he invited me to smoke hookah with them later that night. I accepted excitedly; not having the slightest idea what hookah was, but simply ecstatic to be invited.

True to his restless nature, my dad did not wait for even a moment before herding my mother and brother back into his car, commencing the drive back to South Carolina. As I watched them pull off into the distance, I dreaded the inevitable task before me: spending the remainder of the day organizing my room. While I would have preferred to ask my friends if they were back on campus, I didn't want to be another factor that bothered them in addition to the chaos of move-in day. Luckily, before I was relegated to simply unpacking for the afternoon, I received a message from Charles who had arrived on campus not too long after me. He asked me the very question I was too chicken to ask, and we decided to get everyone together for lunch; maybe check out the new dorms everyone was staying in if we had time.

As I stood outside my building waiting, I noticed someone making a beeline toward me that I didn't recognize. I started to feel uneasy as he picked up his pace, until I realized it was Charles who had gotten a deep tan that left him nearly unrecognizable. I was nervous for our first chat in months, but I was happily surprised when our conversation picked up as if only three days had passed since we last saw each other. The remainder of the day flew by like a whirlwind, revealing to me that all my panicking was needless. We met up with John, visited Nicole, and checked out each other's dorms. It became clear that our friendship didn't depend on a single connecting factor as I feared, and we had indeed formed genuine bonds.

Later that afternoon, I returned to my dorm so I could mentally prepare for the night ahead with my new roommates. I looked at the door with both Lunan and I's names on it and smiled as I opened the door, hoping to see the big ol' bear that helped me to form all of these wonderful friendships. But, of course, the room was vacant; filled only with my bags and the dorm furniture provided by Mason. It was a tough pill to swallow, but Lunan was not going to be returning that year.

I was disappointed, but far from surprised. Lunan had made this disheartening fact very clear over the summer after familial circumstances compelled him to move back to New York City. His name on the door was clearly a mistake made by the resident advisor who hadn't been given an updated list of the students living on his floor. But seeing Lunan's name on the door when I arrived made me believe for a moment that it wasn't true. I needed that hope because I was scared, and I held onto the illusion as tight as I could.

But the day showed me that my friends were really my friends. That we weren't cursed to drift apart as soon as Lunan was gone. It showed me that I also had great suitemates to come back home to, and they were just a bathroom away. There was nothing for me to fear.

Without dwelling on it too long, I walked over to Xavier and Nick's room where I could hear people gathering. What better way to start my sophomore year, than to find my own inner Lunan, walk through that door, and introduce myself to a room full of strangers.

Chapter 5

Running Unabashed

Two purple blurs blitzed through the crowded Mason
sidewalks, making a beeline for the Johnson Center; the four-
story brick building with white facades marking each
entrance that sat in the heart of GMU. Weaving around
students and faculty alike, jumping over benches, and ducking
underneath low hanging branches, the blurs seemed
undeterred by any obstacle. Taking a closer look, one would
notice they were, in reality, royal purple ties flapping
desperately as they trailed the path of the two young black
men that donned them around their necks. As the only pops of
color in an otherwise black outfit of slacks and collared shirts,
they stood out in the night. The young men's eyes burned
with determination while sweat dripped from their brows.
Time was of the essence, and none of it could be wasted on
politely strolling down the walkway. In order to compensate
for their boorishness, the two men yelled "excuse me" and
"sorry" to every person they rushed past. To everyone that

saw their mad dash, it was obvious they were pledges. And those pledges were Xavier and me.

In those moments, no one was more surprised by that fact than myself. There I was, giving my all and putting myself in a situation that required being boisterous. Pouring everything I had into any task, even those I enjoyed, was never my style. It felt uncool. Doing my best would have put me in a vulnerable position. If I used everything I had in the tank and still fell short, I'd be left without any excuse for my failure. I'd be forced to face the reality that I wasn't good enough. That's a hard pill to swallow, especially for someone like myself who was always trying to appear cool, calm, and collected.

Yet for some reason, under the watchful eye of the shimmering stars above, I couldn't care less about how I appeared to any onlookers, nor the fact that I was being forced into this race. It was exhilarating. I could feel this was exactly what I needed in my life. Something to push my boundaries and shake up my world. Even as my dress shoes began to hurt with every step of my run, I couldn't help but smile with elation at the man that ran beside me. It was only thanks to my journey into his room that first night in the dorm, that I was part of such a thrilling scene to begin with.

***

When I entered Xavier and Nick's side of the suite that first night back on campus, I was introduced to Mark and Amanda. Mark was a brother in Nick's fraternity, AKΛ, and they seemed to have relatively similar personalities, though Mark seemed more academically driven, while Nick had shown himself to be more easy-going when it came to studying and due dates.

Amanda was a nice enough girl, but something seemed off about her. She seemed almost purposefully aloof like a horror-movie, blonde bimbo. Xavier told me about his crush on her during our end of the semester hangout, so even though I couldn't see the appeal in her personality at first glance, I told myself there had to be more to her than that.

I was also lucky to make the acquaintance of a girl named Zee. She was Amanda's friend and a student in the same Cornerstone LLC program that Xavier participated in during his freshman year. Looking for some advice from him, she came by to introduce herself. Try as I might to deny it, I had a crush on the girl from the moment I laid eyes on her. She was a gorgeous and voluptuous young black woman whose beauty caused me to sweat bullets while my tongue failed at any attempt to form a proper sentence. Not to mention that despite her short stature, she had the kind of fiery and candid attitude I liked in a girl.

Once everyone had gathered and introduced themselves, we all headed outside for the main attraction of the night: hookah. Watching Xavier put together the strange but regal device piqued my interest, but I didn't plan on smoking. I hated the scent of cigarettes more than anything and assumed the burning of the slimy, goo-like shisha wouldn't smell any more pleasant. The smoking apparatus itself seemed like something you would see in a science lab: a piece of charcoal burned the mushy leaves and produced a haze that rested gently on the water in the reservoir below, until someone inhaled through the long accordion-esque hose, causing the water to bubble and the smoke to flow into some poor fool's lungs. Nothing about hookah seemed healthy, so I decided I would stay only a few minutes and return to my room to avoid being around the toxic fumes too long.

But then as they began to start the "experiment", I became entranced by an intoxicating aroma; a siren's call beckoning me with the promise of satisfying a sweet tooth without any of that pesky sugar. My nose was filled with the smell of gummy bears surfing on fruity hard candies in a punch bowl filled with the saccharine nectar of an orange. My curiosity for the flavor that accompanied such a scent got the best of me and I surrendered myself to the alluring haze.

The smoke was smoother than I expected it would be and I was pleasantly surprised to find it tasted exactly as I imagined. Further dazzled by the size of the clouds that I could breathe in and out, I became fully mesmerized by the peculiar contraption.

Throughout the night, and as I permitted more and more smoke to fill my lungs, mentions of rush events were thrown around the table by Nick and Mark. These were events sponsored by a fraternity or sorority to generate interest in the organization and garner new members. I wasn't the least bit interested, so the conversation became white noise as I focused on how the clouds of smoke I expelled from my lungs rose and dissipated in the night sky. To me, the fraternity world was filled with elitist individuals who felt the privilege of their friendship required testing of the seekers and culling of those unworthy. I fully believed that while bonds could be formed through shared hardship, no genuine connection could possibly form between a victim and their oppressor. Any bond formed between the two would merely wear the mask of friendship and brotherhood. What they truly offered, in my opinion, was tantamount to Stockholm's Syndrome.

So, I kept my head low and smoked hookah until I heard the most beautiful words that had graced my ears in a long time: Room full of trampolines. The kid in me lit up and alarm bells went off in my head. This was not a drill; It was time to put down this delicious candy vapor and speak up. I was on a mission. I needed to get into that rush event, no matter what.

But even after putting the hose down, I was still me. It was difficult to find the perfect words I could say to such a large group of people I had just met, so I ended up remaining silent and doing my best to simply look interested. Hopefully, I'd seem cool enough to be invited to the event in question. Lucky for me, Xavier didn't shy away from the situation and asked for more details at every opportunity. We learned that unlike the fraternities and sororities of The Divine Nine, the recruitment events of social fraternities were open to all students. Xavier nudged me and smirked upon confirming we could attend, and my eyes began to twinkle with excitement; I looked forward to this promise of high-flying fun more than any college party. Noticing that Xavier and I were both interested, Amanda offered to drive us to the event, and we accepted right away.

A week or so later, we arrived at a shabby-looking building that supposedly held enough trampolines to put a bounce house to shame. Since I still had no interest in joining the group, I felt like I was going on a date solely for a free meal. In contrast, Xavier appeared excited to meet the brothers, though he still wasn't fully convinced that the fraternity life was for him. Neither of us were big partygoers or drinkers, so the overall benefits seemed slim.

On the inside, the venue looked more beautiful than I could have ever imagined. There were trampolines as far as the eye could see. Nets lined the front of the bounce areas filled with flat, squared off sections of trampoline that made up the majority of the floor, while trampoline "walls" aligned the edges. I rushed over with Xavier and bounced to my heart's content with stars in my eyes. All felt right with the world. Alas, periodically a brother of the fraternity would bounce his way over in order to introduce himself and start a conversation explaining what their organization was about. Each time, the stars dimmed as I was jerked out of my bliss.

The brothers seemed friendly, but I just couldn't get over the idea that pledging meant hazing, and hazing was something I did not want to be a part of. So as soon as the bouncing hour had come to a close, we were first in line to drop off the protective gear at the front desk. As we tried to skedaddle out of the building without being noticed, a brother caught up with us and handed Xavier an invitation to their bid night dinner; the night where they would select their newest pledges from among the invitees. This invitation wasn't just for Xavier though, but for me as well. For the life of me, I couldn't understand why. Could they not sense my disinterest?

When we all got back into the car, I began joking about how desperate the fraternity must be to include me in their dinner. Not once did I form a connection with any of the brothers I had met that night. Furthermore, I was quiet, reserved, and revolted by everything I had ever heard about the pledge process. I was not what they were looking for.

But then Xavier shocked me by revealing that he was genuinely interested in pledging after talking to Nick and his brothers. On top of that, he was hoping I would join him. He told us that he and the brothers had discussed the personal growth that being in the fraternity had provided them, the business connections one can make, and the lifelong friendships that would be formed through the pledge process and service within the fraternity. This was what Xavier wanted most of all out of his college experience. After being homeschooled for most of his life and attending a tiny Christian academy during his high school years, all he wanted was a group of lifelong friends that he knew would have his back no matter what. His reasoning resonated with me.

While I was still skeptical about pledging, I told Xavier I would attend the bid night dinner if he really wanted to go. I felt like I had to support my friend in this endeavor, especially after he had been so open and inviting toward me.

Or rather, I wanted to offer that support but then have him politely turn me down. My plan didn't include actually going to the dinner and socializing with forty strangers. As the day came closer and closer, I was dreading it and thinking of excuses not to go. *Pretending to be sick? No, that wouldn't work. Too much homework? No, it was too early in the semester for that old excuse. Previous plans? Maybe.*

So, like the genius that I am, I hid at Charles's dorm while pretending my phone had run out of power. Among my friends I had become well known for my phone always dying, so this was definitely the most believable explanation for not replying to his messages. A simple "oh no my phone died, and I forgot all about the dinner" and "I won't be able to make it back in time, leave without me" would seal the deal.

But after telling Charles my plan, he threw me a curveball. He asked me "why not just give it a shot?"

Charles was never the type of person to tell someone what to do. Only offering facts and alternate perspectives, rather than a guiding hand. Sometimes, though rare, he would say what he would do in someone's position. And in my situation he said he would want to go. If my goal was to grow this year, why not face something new to see what I could get out of it? Why not find out if my assumptions about fraternities were true or not? Either I would be proven right and could leave with my pride intact, or they would surprise me. I had nothing to lose.

Hearing that had caught me off guard, so I went to the bathroom to think. I sat on the toilet weighing the pros and cons of my options, but the process only pushed me further and further from a clear decision; one minute I'd be resolved to attend, and the very next, choosing to accede to my more reclusive nature. I felt like I was getting nowhere. Just a few minutes earlier my plan was clear, but now I didn't know. I grew frustrated as I realized that I was truly considering attempting to pledge. *Damnit Charles.*

But then it dawned on me that my prejudice against fraternities wasn't the only thing holding me back. It was fear. A fear of having to host parties. A fear of being forced to embarrass myself in public. A fear of talking to women I considered way out of my league. This realization frustrated me even more. *Why can't I just grow up?*

Then at that moment, in the midst of my inner turmoil, I received a text from Xavier asking if I was still going to the bid night dinner. He and Amanda were going to leave for the restaurant in about fifteen minutes.

I still hadn't made a decision, but the reality of my choices made itself crystalline before me. This wasn't me grappling between going to a dinner or not. No, this choice masked the true decision I was making in my heart. Between adventure and staying comfortable.

Taking a deep breath, I jumped off that toilet, and said a quick goodbye to everyone in Charles' dorm. I dashed across campus to get back to my room so I could change. I didn't have much time, but I knew I couldn't miss out on that dinner. I didn't know if I was making the right choice, but I knew I was tired of being afraid to venture past the known. There is nothing wrong with being comfortable and staying where you are, but fear shouldn't be the reason you choose to stay.

I ran and I ran; feeling out of breath but determined. I was embarrassed, but I had no time to care. I had no time to waste.

***

And there I was, running through campus once again. Now accompanied by Xavier as we burst through the doors of the JC and sprinted toward the campus barbecue spot in order to pick up dinner for the brothers who now commanded our lives. We heard snickers and giggles, but they only fueled us. As we paid for the meal and prepared for our race back to the meet up spot, the cute cashier smiled at me and asked if we were pledges. I gave her a big ole smile as I started to turn away and leave. Replying with a simple and confident "yep," as Xavier and I took off once more.

Chapter 6

Shotgun

It was the morning of October 27, 2012; I laid in bed reflecting on the pledge process and dreading the night to come.

At this point I had been pledging for over a month, and it was hard to tell if my decision to join the fraternity was worth it. And I mean that literally. Having recently paid $300 in dues, my initial excitement began to wane as it dawned on me that I was handing the group my hard-earned cash so I could be put through the grinder.

Within weeks it became clear that some brothers challenged us in order to make us better people through assignments that required teamwork and planning, while others merely treated us like butlers that existed for their amusement. We were made to do anything from hours of taxing labor on lawns that had been long neglected, to breaking into personalized dances at the mention of a single code word regardless of where we were. It didn't take long before the nightly sprints across campus to procure food for our new masters began to lose their luster.

Thankfully I wasn't going through it alone. Besides Xavier and I, there was Brian, Caleb, Trace, and Kyle.

Brian was a tall scrawny white kid from Jersey with a short, scraggly beard and short, greasy hickory-brown hair. He was impulsive, unflappable, and, surprisingly, quite the ladies' man. Few women seemed capable of resisting his silver tongue.

Trace was the biological brother of one of the fraternity brothers, Troy. Oddly enough, Trace was the older one, but he was definitely the nerdier and less mature of the two. He was a big, sensitive, and loveable teddy bear who loved to sleep nearly as much as he loved to paint.

Kyle was the youngest of us and the only freshmen. He also seemed to come from money, if his souped-up car was any clue. He was always ready for a good time, and this typically led to him being quite irresponsible.

And finally, there was Caleb. He was "Murica" incarnate, and proud of it. When he wasn't wearing pledge clothes, it wasn't uncommon to find him wearing full American flag garb. America, guns, booze, and the Republican Party seemed to be his greatest loves. He was a goofy guy that could drink anyone under the table, though he was much more responsible and tame than Kyle or Brian outside of a party environment.

In comparison to our pledge brothers, Xavier and I were both unassuming and inobtrusive. Yet even still, with his natural ability to lead and motivate, Xavier had become our Pledge Class President. This in turn made him our de facto leader in any given situation.

As for me, I was being my typical quiet self and taking the cushy unofficial role as Xavier's second. Typically, I'd only speak briefly during our weekly meetings in order to reinforce or explain Xavier's proposals on how we were going to tackle a given task. This job suited me just fine, especially in the early days when forming a connection with my other pledge brothers revealed itself to be more difficult than I expected. Our personalities just didn't jive and our perspectives on the world couldn't have been more different. If we didn't happen to be a part of the same pledge class, I would have never interacted with them in the first place. Thus, our meetings were the only time I'd bother to chime in, though this was simply to prevent them from devolving into endless discussions and arguments, rather than an attempt to get closer with any of the other pledges.

Thank God that, eventually, the mystical combination of adversity and shared experience worked it's magic and I was able to not only find common ground with my new pledge brothers, but become friends. Navigating the rocky terrain that is the pledge process became more tolerable once I was able to share my gripes concerning how new members were treated, and joke about our self-imposed struggles with everyone. While the process never got any easier, the camaraderie was the sugar that helped the daily dose of exploitation go down.

Sadly, no amount of sugar could help me through the task that awaited me that night. Within less than ten hours, I'd be a costumed valet for our fraternity's Halloween party.

Our job appeared simple at first glance; all we had to do was shuttle guests to and from the house party that our fraternity was holding off campus. But in addition to transporting students to and fro, there was a hidden responsibility to the role. As a pledge you are the face of the fraternity. Everything, from how you dress to the music you play in the car, mentally prepares the rider for the group of people they are going to be partying with. This meant I had to be entertaining, instead of my usual mute self.

Beyond that seemingly insurmountable challenge, I was worried about being judged on my choice of costume. It was the full outfit of a certain green plumber. The package contained a bright green top with navy blue overalls and an equally audacious green cap. Oh, and I would be remiss not to mention the cartoon white gloves and faux mustache that brought the whole ensemble together. At first I was excited to show off this fun and silly costume, but then Xavier decided to dress as the king of cool, Kanye West.

When we tried on our costumes the night before, I looked ridiculous next to him. He looked like the epitome of suave and simple with his black shirt, chain, and shutter shades. I felt like a clown, knowing everyone at the party was going to whisper about the silent weirdo in the Player 2 disguise standing with him.

The mere thought left me frozen in my bed. I continued to keep my eyes shut, refusing to look at the clock as if the time wouldn't start until I stood up to get ready for the day. Part of me hoped that maybe if I continued to believe that I had this small power over time, I could defy it and skip to the next day. But time is no one's to control, and within moments of hearing my door open and shut, a sudden sharp and putrid scent entered my nostrils, hijacked my brain, and compelled my body to jump to its feet.

Standing across from me at the side of his own bed was the champion of Chronos and the source of the stench: my new roommate Bubba who had just come back from the gym. I don't remember too much about Bubba beyond that he was Caucasian, and the messiest person I had ever met. Piles of laundry were always left undone, large cups filled to the brim with chewing tobacco rested uncovered on his desk, and what seemed like discarded sheets of homework were spread across his floor as if he were constantly using them as steppingstones in an unending game of "The Floor is Lava."

He was an amiable man and a student in his final semester at Mason. When he had first moved in as a replacement for Lunan, I had assumed he would be a wealth of knowledge and advice, but his demeanor and personal hygiene matched the garbage dump that was his space in the room, and abated any desire I had to converse with him for more than a few minutes. I couldn't help but look at him with some level of disgust out of the corner of my eye as the odor from his side of the room grew each and every day.

Now fully awake, I threw on my clothes, brushed my teeth, and ran out the door as fast as I could to escape his stink. After using the back entrance to the building and stopping to take a deep breath of fresh air, I walked leisurely to the campus shuttle stop.

In order to make some money to help pay for pledge dues and tuition, I started working at a women's clothing store in the nearby Fair Oaks Mall. Since my car was left behind in South Carolina, I was relegated to taking a long ride on the shuttle that made a stop at the mall. On a good day this trip could take almost an hour, but on a bad one the shuttles were so full I'd have to wait for multiple shuttles to pass before eventually squeezing myself through the crowd and onto one of the few open seats. This meant I had to leave at least two hours ahead of time just in case the first shuttle I tried to get on was filled to capacity. Most days I would loathe this long commute, but today it was my saving grace from Eau de Bubba.

The work at the store itself was neither good nor bad. I just folded clothes in the backroom while listening to music. Occasionally they'd be so desperate for help at the cash registers that they turned to me for assistance, at which point I would awkwardly emerge from my hideout and attempt to sell women's clothing without knowing anything about fashion. The situation made me feel like a flightless bird attempting to peddle airplanes, but it helped to break the monotony of my backroom duties, so I never complained.

My plan was to change into my costume at the end of my shift, sneak out before anyone saw, and hop into Kyle's car so he could take us directly to the party to start our valet duties. But there was one problem. At the beginning of my shift, when I looked into my bag to grab my headphones, I realized I had forgotten the costume. I left my dorm in such a rush, placing it in my bag slipped my mind. Thanks to my blunder, we'd have to make a pitstop back in my room and smell my roommate's perfume once more.

Once my workday had come to an end, my pledge brothers picked me up and we sped down the road toward Mason. Xavier and I used the entirety of the trip to prepare our compatriots for the nearly visible stench of Bubba, trying to make sure they did not associate us with whatever they encountered in the room.

When we arrived at our dorm, we entered through Xavier's door as everyone pinched their nose in order to protect themselves. I made my way through the joint bathroom to my side, slowly opening the door in an attempt to avoid shocking the olfactory systems of my pledge brothers with a sudden surge of funk. But when I opened the door, by some miracle, there wasn't a single vomit-inducing smell to be found. I poked my head through the threshold to see that there was indeed a miracle that had taken place. Bubba cleaned his side of the room. Well, mostly. He still had a pile of clothes and papers laying on the floor, but now they were pushed almost entirely under his bed.

Did he finally realize humans weren't meant to live like this? Did he finally grow concerned about what his roommates thought of him? Maybe his tobacco spit cup became too full for even him to stomach? To be honest, I didn't care about the reason, and I didn't ask. I had no desire to ruin a good thing with questions about the why, so I simply got myself ready and enjoyed the rare smell of a tidy room.

While we got ourselves together, Xavier began to express his own anxiety about the night. He was worried about driving a brother's car and potentially getting into an accident, and said worries were heightened when he thought about caring for his drunk passengers. He also expressed his general anxiety about being a fun person at parties, which made me realize I wasn't alone in our pledge group. We began to commiserate each other's feelings and moan and groan about the night until we were interrupted by Bubba. He had returned during our prep and overheard our conversation, which caused him to do something I didn't see coming. He gave us advice. It was nothing particularly profound, but it still had an impact. He told us to "Just have fun no matter what." He also tried to give us some slightly questionable advice on how to pick up girls that we immediately put in the mental garbage bin, but I like to focus on the good.

"Have fun no matter what."

For whatever reason that caused something to click in my head. I was overthinking. I was stopping myself from enjoying the night before it even began. So now, while donning my mustache and one-size-fits-all plumber garb, I promised myself I would enjoy the night.

I came up with a plan to make it as easy as possible to achieve that goal. The first step of which was to eliminate the biggest stressor that night: driving. So, I "forgot" my glasses in the dorm as we left for the night and prevented myself from being able to legally driving. And though I'd be unable to take the wheel, I still planned to ride shotgun alongside Xavier in order to make sure everything went smoothly as he ferried partygoers. The frequent breaks from the wall-thumping music and merriment would also bless my brain with an opportunity to cool down and recharge before my social batteries were fully drained.

When we arrived at the house to help set up for the party, I initiated my plan by proclaiming, just loud enough for the brothers to hear, that I had forgotten glasses. Since Xavier and I were using a brother's car to shuttle partygoers, the brothers accepted my inability to drive without any fuss and assigned me as Xavier's shotgun as planned. With that covered, I just had to figure out how I was going to get around my other source of stress, and my greatest obstacle: My low self-esteem and social anxiety.

Of course, those weren't going away any time soon, so a few shots of liquid courage and a cup of jungle juice would have to do the trick. I downed a few drinks, hoping it would be just enough to feel the warmth envelope both my body and mind; lending me the undeserved level of confidence I sought.

But before I could even feel the results of my vodka heavy concoctions, Xavier and I were told to go out and pick up a few bottles of soda and juice for the party. It was my time to shine whether I was ready or not. And shine I did.

Xavier and I went to some supermarket that was close to the house and as soon as we got out of the car, the worst-case scenario I had made up in my head occurred. Some inebriated jackass peered out his friend's car and yelled "Where's Mario?" while laughing and pointing in my direction. Anthony from a few months ago would have shrunk and slinked into the store. But something was different this time. It didn't bother me. It didn't even register as an insult.

Maybe it was the drinks I had thrown down my gullet before running this errand, but even alcohol had never before given me the feeling I had at that moment. Something felt fundamentally different within me. I just didn't care about what they had to say. I raised my arms to my side and, while staring down the car as it passed, I yelled "Screw Mario."

And the rest of the night took off from there. Whether it was holding conversations while Xavier drove inebriated college kids to and from the party or stomping the competition in the age-old game of flip cup, I wasn't worried about my appearance or how people perceived me. Not even one bit. It wasn't just me either. Xavier, despite being the sober one, had become the life of the party during our drives. Every passenger left the vehicle either laughing their heart out or flirting with Xavier as they stepped out. The night couldn't have gone better. Even when the fraternity brothers yelled our passcodes and we had to dance in front of the whole party, it was fun. Moving Like Bernie in front of everyone never felt so good.

In fact, during my dance, I had a revelation. All of the embarrassing stuff we were made to do around campus had somehow desensitized me to the gaze of others that would normally have me shying away like a scared turtle. Not to the point that I could go wild in public of my own volition, but enough so that onlookers didn't bother me if I was doing something that was normal. Like dancing at a party. It was small, but it was the first fruit I had truly seen grow from this long, embarrassing, and mentally draining process.

Around four in the morning, I went home with Xavier after we had dropped off our last passengers, and we talked about how proud we were of ourselves. We did it. We enjoyed the night despite all the negative thoughts we had filled our heads with.

Upon entering my side of the suite, I saw a pair of wide doe-eyes staring back at me through the darkness. My eyes adjusted and I could make out the shape of a clearly naked and largely uncovered woman lying next to Bubba. She stared at me unblinking and perfectly still; as if she was painted onto the sheets. I guess Bubba's methods of seduction worked after all.

I was too tired to feign that I hadn't seen her; all I wanted was to get in my bed. So, while averting my eyes the entire time, I gave her a quick handwave to acknowledge her existence, threw off my costume and jumped onto my squeaky dorm mattress. I giggled to myself as I fell asleep, thinking *I was the plumber tonight, but Bubba was the one who got to lay the pipe.*

Chapter 7

The Ties That Bind

Hell Week: the final stretch before a pledge is officially initiated into the fraternal brotherhood. A time that pledges both await eagerly and anticipate in horror as it grows closer. For while it precedes the dawn of brotherhood, this twilight of the pledge process brings with it a wave of sleep deprivation, exhausting labors, and endless errands. It's a true test of limits that brings to light the motivations of a pledge class, the quality of their teamwork, and most importantly the strength of their kinship. The logic behind it was simple. If a pledge class had gone through the adversity of the entire process and failed to develop a sense of brotherhood within their own ranks, how can they be expected to do so once they had been brought into the fold?

At least that was what I told myself. The joyous smile that crossed the brother's faces whenever it was mentioned hinted at a more sinister motive behind this week of torment, but I did my best to ignore it.

It was early November, and we knew the final weeks of pledging had to be upon us. We had been put through many trials and tribulations throughout the semester, and we thought we had done rather well. From tasks as simple as painting a rock for AKΛ in the same vein as the other fraternity rocks that could be found around GMU's campus, to the tortuous feast that was Hot Dog Night, we conquered every challenge and grew closer to one another with each one. But that was where it ended for me.

Unlike my pledge brothers, I was unable to form any sort of bond with any of the brothers of our fraternity. Acquaintanceship maybe, but I couldn't say I felt anything between me and them that was anywhere near the realm of true brotherhood. All the hours spent partying with them couldn't compare to even the dullest moments spent with Xavier. Having gone through many highs and lows together in the short time I had known him, we had developed a close bond that was only matched by my friendship with Charles.

The most shining example of this was when Xavier and I took an online mental health screening quiz. I can't recall why we decided to undergo the questionnaire. The reason must have been somewhere between the dark jokes of self-harm we recounted only to each other and our anxieties concerning the future that we confessed to only when no one else was around. Regardless of what it may have been, we took the test and the results stated that Xavier and I possibly suffered from mild to moderate depression and suggested we see a professional to be properly diagnosed.

For a moment we sat in silence, staring at our screens in disbelief. Finally, I responded by simply yelling out a quick and elongated "Nah!" while slapping my laptop shut. I asserted that the test wasn't meant for a realist such as myself, and I joked that depression was for white people who didn't know how good they had it. My only issue was that I knew the realities of the world I called home. We laughed and Xavier agreed; we couldn't possibly be depressed. He admitted that he may have had some problems he hid from the world before, but his new friends helped take him out of that funk.

There was no way our results could be correct. We continued to chortle while making uncouth jokes about what it would be like if we were really depressed. We laughed until we were gasping on the floor for air; the thought of dying from laughter only exacerbated the situation. The cackling only ended after Xavier crawled over to his room in an attempt to escape from this lethal comedy routine and catch his breath. Once he returned, we both looked at my ocean blue laptop and grew silent once more. After a few seconds we looked at each other and made a pact: if one of us were to ever feel the hefty weight of depression on them, the other would be there to help lift it before it became too much to bear.

While never to the level of what I shared with Xavier, there was also a connection I had with my other pledge brothers that I knew I would never share with the other members of the fraternity. Every day we tried to help each other improve, whether it was related to the fraternity or not.

We all tried to help Brian quit smoking cigarettes. We all took shifts to ensure that Trace, famous for sleeping through anything important, woke up on time for any fraternity events and his classes. Brian and Xavier even did their best to help me work up the courage to ask out Zee, going as far as to make a deal where if I confessed my feelings to Zee, Xavier would do the same with Amanda. We'd all joke about how the worst that could happen is that one of us would end up crying in the Swagger Wagon; a royal purple and gold children's wagon with our fraternity's letters, AKΛ, painted on the side. It was the most prized heirloom of our chapter; one that had been handed down from pledge class to pledge class for years.

So, when we attended our weekly pledge meeting in early November, I was taken aback when they told us they didn't believe we were anywhere near ready to be initiated into their organization. In spite of how close we had become, they felt our dedication was lacking, our motivation moreso, and our honest efforts were muddied by our terrible teamwork. Worst of all, they felt our priorities were not in the right place, and as consequence some of us were even failing multiple courses. In the same vein, they accused those of us with passing grades of regularly choosing to ignore our pledge duties, while still enjoying the parties and social events held by the fraternity.

This was quite the disconcerting news. Not just because it meant that we may have wasted an entire semester running errands and being made fools of, but also because their accusations were partially true. I personally questioned my motivations every day of this process. I was only there for the challenge to begin with. I never held any personal stake in whether or not I made it into the fraternity. At worst it was a waste of $300. Furthermore, I was indeed guilty of shirking my duties under the guise of homework or work so I could relax away from the fraternity and spend some time with the old Eisenhower Crew.

As I looked around the room, I could tell by their downcast gazes that the criticism rang true for my pledge brothers as well. Xavier had always felt he wasn't able to execute his duties as Pledge Class President quite up to snuff. Since he never liked to yell, he often had a hard time reeling us all in once we had broken into shouting arguments. Brian, Caleb, and Kyle were well aware of the fact that they prioritized the fun aspects of pledging over the tedious tasks that were given; often leading to the arguments Xavier failed to calm. When it came to Trace, even with our efforts to act as his alarm clocks later in the process, he had already missed so many meetings that it had caught the eyes of the brothers. In the end, we were all partially at fault for our current predicament.

The criticism continued for the majority of the meeting, and I slowly became offended for my pledge brothers. They wanted this more than anything. It didn't seem right that they may be punished for what I considered small infractions. Especially since the brothers had often been encouraging them in the moments they were committed, or turning a blind eye as they watched our group fall short of expectations.

As I began to grind my teeth out of frustration, prepared to rise to my pledge brothers' defense, our New Member Educators, Sam and Troy, revealed our saving grace. They liked us. And thanks to that, they were giving us one week to prove we had the skills and drive worthy of becoming members of AKΛ. They announced Hell Week was upon us, and it started the following week.

Everyone's eyes lit up at this opportunity, like a child offered a chance of redemption after disappointing their parents. The six of us left that room full of hope, while discussing how we needed to change our approach if we were going to survive the flames of the week ahead. The vibe of the group was different; the determination to be initiated into the brotherhood oozed from every pore of the five men walking with me as they discussed strategies for combating anything the brothers threw at us. Even if I didn't care if I personally made it to initiation day, I would do my best to help us all make it there so we could stand together as brothers.

Later that night, in need of some relaxation, Xavier suggested we have some of our recently invented Special Hookah. Watered-down mango juice with ice instead of the usual-flavorless water and Pirate's Cave shisha mixed with a very special secret ingredient.

Ever since that first day of smoking hookah, I learned how habit forming it could really be. Whenever Xavier or I felt particularly stressed, we would set up the hookah and enjoy the quickly fading high that the thick, white tobacco smoke provided. Eventually we experimented with mixing different flavors and replacing the water to improve the taste and smoothness of the smoke we desperately craved. Eventually Nick had suggested we add a certain ingredient from his personal collection, and Special Hookah was born.

Knowing Charles wouldn't want to miss out on our favorite new pastime, I invited him over. We decided to set up shop on a picnic table behind one of the student union buildings at GMU. On our way, we stopped at the convenience store downstairs from our dorm and picked up the juice we needed, along with a chocolate bar that caught my eye due to its elongated, pyramid-like shape. I had heard tales of this legendary triangle chocolate bar and its decadent flavor for years, and the hunger Special Hookah imposed on us seemed like the perfect excuse to give it a try.

As we sat down and the coals began to burn away at the shisha, Xavier and I could feel our stress floating away with every stream of smoke we blew at the sky. My body felt light, as if pledging and classes were merely a nightmare my brain had concocted; like this moment in time was all that existed. Then, as Xavier and Charles shared their plans for the upcoming Thanksgiving break, a wave of melancholy swept me away.

My vacation request for Black Friday was denied by my boss at the mall, meaning there was no way I would be able to go home for Thanksgiving. This would be my first experience away from my family during the holidays, let alone the first one I was going to spend entirely alone in an empty dorm. Charles, noticing the grim look on my face, asked me what was on my mind. Allowing a fluffy column of vapors to escape my lips as I spoke, I told them about how lonely I felt knowing that in two weeks almost everyone on campus was going to be at home with their families, enjoying a big meal and a day off, while I sat alone in my dorm rifling through old mail to find a menu from the nearby Chinese restaurant that I prayed to God would be open so I could eat something warm that didn't come from the microwave. Then there was the fact that I had no idea how I was going to get to work since the shuttle system at Mason wasn't going to be operating over the holiday weekend.

After hearing me vent, without skipping a beat and very matter-of-factly, Charles invited me to his home for the holidays. The look on his face was nonchalant; as if I should have known all along that I'd be staying with him for the biggest food holiday in the country. As if we had made these plans months ago. But I was stunned by the offer. I had never been invited to a friend's home for the holidays before.

I was so touched it may have brought me to tears if I didn't notice the campus police officer rounding the Student Union Building and walking in our direction. I covertly gestured at him while staring at my fellow ne'er-do-wells with fear in my eyes. After they too became aware of his presence, we immediately entered panic mode. He turned his head toward us and slowed his pace, appearing to gauge the situation at hand. We needed to act naturally. We searched for our phones, but it turned out that while we were so busy remembering to bring every part of the intricate hookah, we had forgotten them in the dorm.

As the campus policeman approached, he glared over to our table with laser-like focus. He held the gaze for what felt like minutes. To the point where we swore he knew what we were doing. There was no time left, we had to do something to throw off his suspicion before he managed to get too close. So, in our best inebriated judgment, we began reading the nutrition facts on the back of the chocolate I had purchased earlier.

What proceeded was the most ingenious improv to have ever been performed. We moved closer to each other and noticeably grimaced at the number of calories per bar. Next we exclaimed loudly, with surprise, at the amount of sugar and fat. Then I opened the chocolate and we each took some and savored it in our mouths. We started to praise the taste of the decadent confection while discussing how something so luscious and mouthwatering couldn't possibly be so bad for one's health.

All this went on while the campus policeman strolled up to the spot in the sidewalk right in front of our table. We didn't dare look at him directly even once since we had started our acting routine, so we had no idea what the look on his face was. What we did know was that he stopped only feet away from us, shook his head, and went on his way without saying a word. As we watched him move out of sight and into the night, we sat quietly awaiting the moment we knew we were in the clear. As soon as we could no longer see him, we extinguished the coals and packed up our things within minutes.

Chuckling and chortling the whole way home, we couldn't help but feel a sense of accomplishment for our quick thinking. We may not have been in the running for any awards for our acting, but we certainly gained a story we would tell for a lifetime. The type of story you tell your friend's children when they can't believe their dad was ever that wild. We knew we had gained a tale that would bond us for life. One that we would tell at each other's weddings.

Not long after we made it back to the dorm, Xavier fell asleep while relaxing in his bed. As he snored in the background, Charles and I decided to call it a night. As he left and the door started to swing shut behind him, I jumped up and ran to catch it. Poking my head through the threshold, I asked Charles if it was really okay for me to intrude on his family's Thanksgiving. He smiled and told me "Of course." Elated, I officially accepted the offer and let the door close. Thanks to our little brush with danger, I felt energized and refreshed. I knew I could handle anything hell week would throw at me.

***

"I was wrong. I was so wrong. The magnitude of my ignorance and poor judgement will be written down and recounted to my family for generations as a cautionary tale."

This was all that went through my mind as a bright red stream of projectile vomit flew out of my mouth, taking my naive self-assurance along with it. Despite the cold air, I was drenched in sweat; my legs were trembling, and my stomach couldn't handle any more of the abuse it had been put through. As I wiped my mouth with the back of my hand, I looked behind to see that my pledge brothers were still trailing behind me on the track. I had just finished the famous Beer Mile, though one could argue that I hadn't since I had refused to drink alcohol on a night before classes. In its stead, I was given a case of Gatorade, but upon reaching my second lap of the race I learned why the brothers weren't too perturbed about accommodating me. The alcohol was a mere red herring. It was the unbearable amount of liquid in your gut that made the run a challenge.

Xavier finished after me with Caleb and Kyle close behind. Trace and Brian were the worst off, as they were nowhere near finishing. Brian being a heavy smoker and Trace being a bigger guy did them no favors. We cheered them on as best we could, even as they both stopped to vomit again and again. We could tell what they were thinking from their body language. They were ready to give up. No, more accurately they had already done so.

The four of us who had finished were standing with the brothers who had been watching us suffer around the track. Brian still had a half lap to go, while Trace had barely started his third. The air was tense as we saw our two pledge brothers come to a halt. We looked at each other, grimacing at the idea, but knowing what had to be done. We hustled back onto the track. First tailing Brian and helping him to finish his final stretch, and then making our way to Trace to help push him to the end of his own run. Though his final lap felt unending, Trace eventually reached the finish line and we all collapsed on the turf surrounding the track. We were exhausted but proud, foolishly thinking we had finally completed our first night of hell week.

The brothers briefly congratulated us before proceeding to drag us to one of their houses and forcing us to sit in a crawl space. Our orders were simple: learn everything we could about each other.

Feeling we knew each other pretty well, we decided to review the basics: favorite colors, political affiliations, and all of the other dull ice breaker questions. The conversation eventually grew into so much more. Caleb shared wild tales of guns, family and the desert back in Arizona. Xavier detailed his history with betrayal and insecurity back in Richmond. I myself shared a haunting narrative of the recurring dream I had been experiencing at least once a year since I was in middle school.

Everyone listened attentively as I chronicled the dream that would start like any normal day, but quickly evolve into something more mystical when an enchantingly beautiful girl would transfer to my homeroom that morning. She would be about my height and have a slim build. Her bone straight black hair fell to her shoulder blades, giving way to a stunning violet dress. She had vibrant, amber-colored skin that complimented her misty grey eyes that pierced straight through my heart. I would be so captivated that I would run up to her after class in the crowded halls to introduce myself, only to be greeted by a mischievous smile containing pointed, shark-like teeth. I'd notice the halls were dead silent, and, upon taking a quick glance around to confirm my fears, they were now empty. I'd turn to run, sensing the ill intentions of the siren, only to fall into a deep black hole along the way. I'd wake up in the mouth of a cave. The only thing obstructing my view of the world outside was a large crag pointed toward the entrance. Standing atop it was the girl. Her dress now ripped and the skin of her face beginning to slough off. She would remove the decaying skin to reveal a sickly grey hide and matted, olive-green hair filled with white streaks. She appeared emaciated; all of her bones clearly visible through her skin. Her rows of fangs were now hidden behind a smug and superior look on her face. She'd raise both of her hands, holding them palms up as if she were carrying a large platter. Swirling smoke trails appeared in her palms, forming shapes my mind failed to comprehend; I'd stare at her face wondering what she could possibly desire. The dream would go completely silent, as if I had lost my hearing entirely, as she offered me a choice. I could never hear my options, but I felt them in my spirit. Even though my mind still failed to make sense of what she held in her palms, something in my soul knew they took the forms of my choices. I'd be filled with such an all-consuming terror by this silent ultimatum that I would force myself awake, refusing to answer the question.

As we tried to decipher the possible meaning of the nightmare, after what felt like hours, the brothers finally let us out. Those of us that had projects or homework due soon were allowed to work on them, but we were never allowed a moment's rest. All my memories of the remainder of that night bleed together. An amalgamation of lightning round questioning about each of my pledge brothers and learning how to create a website for IT class. The only clear memory was of the following morning, when I finally arrived in the lecture room for my IT course. As soon as I took my seat in the back, exhaustion covered me like a warm blanket, and my vision became foggy. With every blink, I could feel my consciousness fade. My will was slipping by the minute. Not even fifteen minutes into the lesson, my eyelids closed like curtains marking the end of a show.

Chapter 8

Stoking the Flame

Anger and disgust grew within me as I stood there shaking, smoking a disposable hookah pen vigorously as I struggled to calm down. My blood boiled as I reread the message from The President:

"Watch what you say, or you may not make it to initiation."

That was it. I was done. I no longer wanted to join this fraternity.

I quit.

How could a person be so out of touch that they feel that was the proper response to my original message? How high do you have to be on your own imaginary power that you

believe you can order someone to spit in the face of th
suffering and abuse of other human beings? But I am g
ahead of myself.

Part of our duty as pledges was to interview all of the
brothers. It made sense; you should get to know all the
members in a group before you decide to join their ranks and
call them family. Out of all of the brothers, the interview with
our chapter president was my least favorite. It was a week or
so before Hell Week; Xavier and I decided to do our interview
with The President at the same time since the due date for
completing our interviews was fast approaching, and we both
still hadn't met with him. At first, we had looked forward to it.
We'd only ever interacted with him a few times at parties, but
everyone seemed to love it each time he made the effort to
show his face.

Unfortunately, he turned out to be a macho,
narcissistic atheist with a superiority complex that laughed in
the face of any religion and their believers. He gave off the
vibe of someone who only looked after himself; seeking to
boost himself up under the guise of friendship and good will.
He laughed jeeringly at the Judeo-Christian principles of our
fraternity during the interview, making it very clear he
thought religion was for dullards and the weak minded.
Money and influence seemed to be all that mattered to him
while we spoke. With every question we asked, it became
clear that this man did not belong at the top of our fraternal
hierarchy. On paper he was a model human being: He was
smart, responsible and incredibly fit, but when it came to his
spirit and the source of his drive, he disgusted me.

Was this a front? Perhaps an act to mess with the newest potential members? I would never come to know. What I do know is that his tone and accompanying expressions were enough to convince me that he was, ironically, telling God's honest truth. Xavier and I left that interview bewildered. How could a person that seems so perfect on the outside, be so rotten on the inside? His words were like noxious fumes betraying the decay of his soul. I left that meeting certain of one thing: The President would never earn my respect.

After enduring forty-eight sleepless hours bouncing between class and pledge tasks, we received a message telling us we had to complete a night-time scavenger hunt through D.C. Each of us were given different locations and monuments with stunts that had to be performed in front of them; video or photographic proof would be provided to the brothers the next morning as evidence. Reading what was in store for us left us all relieved. This task seemed like the easiest. The worst that could happen is that we learned how to navigate the city. Right?

I began to look forward to what seemed like a break in comparison to the other labors of Hell Week, until my eyes reached the end of my list of destinations. It read: "perform pledge dance at the Holocaust Museum." I was taken aback. The shame I felt simply picturing myself "Moving Like Bernie" in front of halls dedicated to tortured souls made me nauseous.

I had to show my pledge brothers what I had read to make sure that I was reading it correctly. The very idea was so abhorrent I couldn't believe it was true. It must have been the lack of sleep causing me to imagine the worst. But the scowls on their faces told me that my sleep deprived brain wasn't dreaming things up. The vein in my forehead began to pulsate as I grew more and more upset, and though I had no proof, I could picture The President laughing as he suggested this sick act.

Quickly, I sent a text to Sam and Troy, along with a few other brothers, telling them that I was not going to commit such a disgusting act. It was too disrespectful. This wasn't about being a good person. This was just the bare minimum of common decency you can show to a place filled with memories of so much pain.

I expected the brothers' response to be uniform. I expected to be told that such a request shouldn't have been made in the first place. Hell, I expected an apology for someone thinking I had the constitution to even consider doing such a thing.

But what I received was mixed messages. Some brothers wondered how the deed even made it on to the list, others told me it wasn't so bad, and even worse yet, many brothers didn't care enough to reply. Still, as I continued to defend my position, I was calm. I was starting to give them the benefit of the doubt. No one was twisting my arm about it, so I began to believe it was simply the fraternity testing a pledges integrity by baiting them into doing something stupid. That is, until the illusion was shattered when I received a message from The President that made it very clear I was nothing more to him than a run of the mill pledge and as replaceable as a number 2 pencil.

It read: "Know your place, or you may not make it to initiation."

Know your place? I was livid. I may not be the most confident person in the world, but if there is one thing that my parents instilled in me, it is self-respect. Who did our president think he was? With his false power and sitting on his throne of pyrite, he somehow believed himself to be superior. I was not here to join a fraternity. That was just an added benefit. I joined for a challenging experience and to support Xavier. I didn't need this pledge process anymore if it was going to push me to go against not only my values, but the very principles the group was formed around.

So, with the hot temper I inherited from my mother, my calm demeanor melted away and I told the brothers exactly how I felt about The President and a fraternity under such repulsive leadership. I promised myself I wouldn't do anything that compromised my values during the pledge process, and this was the moment to either stick to my guns or obey like a dog.

As the discussion continued, I began to realize what I was risking. What if this drove a wedge between me and my pledge brothers? What if I lost the people that made the pledge process worth it? What if even Xavier decided to stop associating with me over this because he had known Nick longer? My hands started to sweat, and I felt like I was beginning to choke. Growing tearful, I clenched my fist and began to hate my situation even more. *Why do all the new friendships I made this semester have to be put at risk?* I wondered. *Over a stupid pledge task? Why--*

And then, as if sensing my anxiety, Xavier placed his hand on my shoulder, and I looked up. His eyes looked disappointed, and he swallowed as if he had a knot in his throat. As if he wished he never had to say what he was going to say next. I braced myself for the worst. I knew he had been looking forward to joining a brotherhood long before I had even met him. I couldn't blame him for choosing to continue the process. Who was I to drag him down with me?

But then, he looked me in my eyes and told me, "We're with you man. We're brothers." My mouth dropped as I stared back; my eyes shifting as I read the kind but resolute look on his face. Glancing past him, I could see Kyle and the rest of our pledge class nodding in agreement. I was ecstatic that my brothers would be by my side, and having their support relieved me of all the stress that was on my shoulders.

Now I had nothing to make me second guess my decision. I knew for sure I would not budge; my character was more important than any organization.

An hour or so after the message from The President, we were asked to come by the largest gym at Mason at the edge of the campus, the RAC. I was still fuming since none of the brothers had confronted him for what he had said, but I couldn't help but smile in the face of what was to come. I imagined that I would be told that I was kicked out of the fraternity and that I could go home while the others went on to do the scavenger hunt in D.C. I was reveling in my fantasies where my pledge brothers would then say that they were going to leave with me, as I smirked at the shocked faces of every member of our chapter. Imagining the brothers' faces of regret as they realized they'd lost an entire pledge class brought me more joy than I could ever express.

When we finally arrived at the gym, the mood among the few brothers present was fraught with tension. Smiling in hopes of cutting through it, Sam and Troy let us know that they still wanted us to do the scavenger hunt in D.C. Predicting my retort, Troy shot me a quick glance. "Don't worry," he stated while letting out a deep sigh. He informed us that we would not be expected to go to the Holocaust Museum, and that performing my dance at any location not already on our list would be enough.

They told us that my status as a pledge was no longer at risk, and that no one would have allowed the dismissal of a pledge that was standing up for what was right. If I still wanted to join the fraternity, I was still their pledge.

I can't remember if I replied, but I remember being put at ease by what we were told. While I was now well aware that not every brother in AKΛ was worthy of my respect, it soothed my heart to know that many of the brothers must have fought to keep me as a pledge - enough to make The President concede. Enough that I thought maybe our pledge class could change this fraternity for the better from the inside. We'd work to eliminate the leadership that simply laughed in the face of the ideals of our founders and bring respect back to the Beta Chi Chapter of AKΛ.

I decided if I wasn't being forced out, I would stick with my pledge class like they stuck by me. That night we went to D.C. using Kyle and Trace's cars. First we would tackle the monuments we had to visit as a group, and then we would separate into two teams based on whose assigned locations were the closest to each other. This ranged from minor monuments, to government buildings, to even the famous Ben's Chili Bowl.

Since I was edging closer and closer to seventy-two hours without sleep, most of my memories from that night are muddied; a grotesque chimera of faint echoes and vague experiences with no discernable beginning, middle, or end. It was a night full of excitement, exhaustion, and frustration.

Laughter rang through the night when we enjoyed each other's company. Yelling took its place whenever we became frustrated due to our unrested minds inhibiting us from finding our destinations quickly. Eventually the yelling vanished, being replaced with silent crying and the solemn desire to go home and be in bed.

Near the end of our hunt, Xavier, Trace, and I ended up in Chinatown. It was early in the morning, and we were starving. Spying a lit open sign in the window of a distant restaurant, we ran over hoping to secure a quick bite before finishing our lists. Upon entering though, we were greeted with an abrupt "We are closed!" I was frustrated and dejected since I saw a few people eating at the tables, but we left without a word to avoid causing a scene.

The encounter shattered the last bit of good morale our trio had for the night. Even though we only had one or two places left on our list, we decided we couldn't go on any longer without food. We unanimously voted to make our way to the nearest late-night burger joint and finally fill our stomachs.

Once we arrived we noticed it was filled to the brim with homeless men and women. We were dumbfounded to see so many and began to wonder if we should go inside. It seemed in bad taste for three goofy college kids complaining about their empty bellies to go into what was apparently a nighttime homeless sanctuary. But our privileged hunger took over and we decided to intrude anyway. Before we could reach the counter, in a sudden and booming voice, the lone cashier yelled that he couldn't take credit cards at that time, and that we would have to get cash from the ATM that was across the street and half a block down the road.

We were so close to sustenance we could already taste the melted cheese and chopped onions. Unable to resist the cries from our bellies, we turned back and started heading outside for the ATM. This revealed the alert and watching eyes of the men and women in the restaurant who had obviously heard the announcement. The sleep deprivation and hunger must have been getting to me, because I swore I heard ominous whispers coming from the crowd. The room began to spin as shadows schemed in the darkness just out of view. Only thanks to Trace yelling "Ant!" was I shaken out of my daze. Still plagued by paranoia, I hurried over to him and Xavier at the door.

The ATM was on a dark sidewalk only illuminated by a single light shining overhead. While Xavier withdrew some money, I still wasn't feeling quite right. Again, I began to feel paranoid that someone would take advantage of the situation. The imaginary alley-way robber my mind conjured up couldn't resist such perfect targets: three exhausted, hungry, and lost college students. Nothing could have made me happier in that moment than when I saw Xavier finally holding the money in his hands. As we crossed the street, and moved past our car, my mind gave in. I felt like my brain was breaking and my body felt like it would follow suit. I begged Trace to open his car so I could rest inside until we were ready to head out and find the rest of our group. I'd reached my limit.

I sat down in the front passenger seat of the car, trying to stay awake, but failing miserably. Despite my eyes being open the whole time, I was in and out of consciousness. With my phone dead and not being very certain of how long I had been alone in the car, I decided to look out the window to see if they were returning with the food. At which point I witnessed a dark figure standing in front of my window, reaching for the door handle. Before I could comprehend what I was seeing, I heard the door to the backseat open abruptly. I began to panic, thinking I was being robbed. I turned slowly, shaking from the fear and praying to God that I would live through the night, only to realize it was Xavier and Trace with burgers in hand. Noticing their faces were clearly confused by my fearful reaction, I returned my attention to the passenger window. But there was no assailant. Only a parking meter.

My mind must be slipping. I thought. With that moment of hysteria over, I closed my eyes and let sleep take over as Xavier started the engine.

The next day I awoke, happy to finally have received some rest and even happier to see that we had all made it back safely. I don't remember when we had reunited with Caleb, Kyle, and Brian, but there they were sleeping on the floor in Xavier and Nick's room along with the rest of us. Following their snore-filled example, I laid back down and took advantage of the rare reprieve.

***

Fast forward to the sixth day of Hell Week, we were standing outside our usual spot where the brothers would pick us up anytime they didn't want us to know where we were being taken. We were brimming with determination to finish the week strong. Finally, we had made it all the way to the end of this antiquated tradition, the experiences of which gave us insight into the factions within the group, the leaders that were failing the whole, and the faulty organization within the chapter. All circumstances that would, one day, drive our chapter into eventual ruin.

My pledge brothers and I discussed all the roles we wanted to fill in the fraternity, as well as the changes we wanted to bring to it. Updates to the pledge education program, better planning for philanthropy events, and nurturing accountability were at the top of our lists. Our goal was to revolutionize the group and return dignity to the Beta Chi name. We wanted our pledge class, Kappa Class, to be the one that turned everything around for the group. We pictured ourselves a year later being the executives of our chapter, ruminating over how we saved our fraternity.

Our musings were interrupted by the sound of the van we had become oh 'so familiar with. We filed into the egg white vehicle and were told immediately to take our ties and make them into blindfolds. Without a single thought, we did as we were told. What was once a concerning request at the beginning of the semester had become customary. I took comfort knowing they had never put us in immediate danger before, and assumed they had no intentions of changing that at the end of the process.

As we were driven to God-knows-where, we were hit with lightning round questions about the fraternity. "Name the founders! Recite the creed! What year was our chapter founded?" The questions were fired one after the other until the van stopped, and we were ordered to file out.

The brothers lined us up and told us we would be hiking through the woods, blindfolded and guided by a few brothers walking the path ahead of us. We were made to also carry the trunk of a small, fallen tree that measured at least seven feet long and was about as thick as a bottle of Gatorade is tall. Despite the six of us holding it together, it was heavy as hell. The log served a dual purpose: helping our group to stay in a single file line the entire time and transforming an otherwise leisurely stroll into something much more laborious. Not knowing where we were, or why we were there, we followed the voices of the brothers through the rocky terrain filled with fallen branches that crunched beneath our feet and weeds that rose up to our calves.

The journey seemed endless while blindfolded. We had no idea how far we were traveling on foot, and the only things that gave a clue to the amount of time passing were the songs we were required to sing as we marched. Cartoon themes, commercial jingles, and even the Campfire Song Song. You name it, we sang it.

Over time the trunk on our shoulders grew heavier and heavier. We stopped occasionally to switch sides; sometimes even resorting to holding it with our hands to give them some rest. Every now and again one of us would trip, causing everyone to fall and drop the log; forcing the group to blindly collect ourselves and our wooden burden as we regained our posture and balanced it back on our shoulders.

Eventually the brothers ordered us to halt, and we were permitted to remove our blind folds. We weren't quite at our destination, but our fumbling along the way had caused the brothers to doubt our ability to complete the next stretch of the trek safely with only their voices as a guide. Thus, they decided we could use our eyes during what was sure to be the most harrowing leg. What laid before us was a small, nearly dry ravine. There was a cliff side to our left, with enough footing for one person to shimmy across. The fall couldn't have been more than ten or so feet; enough to hurt yourself if you weren't careful, but not enough to cause any serious injury.

We all shimmied our way across, one by one, making our way to the hand of one of the brothers who would help us up to the small ridge at the end. I was in my usual spot, second to cross behind Xavier. Waiting on the rest of my pledge brothers to make it across, I looked out into the dark forest as far as I could see. If there was a destination out there, I sure as hell couldn't see it. Only the flashlights the brothers had brought with them provided any light to pierce through the shadowy forest.

I grew slightly worried about what was going on and how much time had passed. It seemed like we had been trekking through the forest for no less than an hour already, with no signs of turning around.

"Blindfolds on!" The command flew as soon as the last of our pledge brothers crossed the small ravine and I rushed to put on my blindfold instinctively.

The rest of the walk was more of the same, only now we were free from our fallen friend whom we had left behind on the other side of the ravine. Based on the whispers of the brothers, we were way behind schedule, and they were growing more and more excited to get the rest of the night started. I could hear the relief and joy in their voices as we seemed to be approaching our destination. They advised us to be careful as we approached a steep downward slope. The sound of a river could be heard in the background, and I could see a faint warm light through my blindfold. We were there.

The brothers lined us up directly in front of the warm light and it seemed like the night was about to truly begin. The heat from the light betrayed the roaring fire it came from. We stood there waiting, hearing only the burble of the water behind us, the crackling of fire in front of us, and the murmurs surrounding us that were muffled by a light but constant breeze.

Finally, the brothers raised their voices to speak; they gave us one simple command. They wanted to hear us recite the creed of ΑΚΛ. In unison the six of us sang out the creed into the night. Our voices echoed through the woods as if they were being carried on the wind itself. Our passion felt evident. As we yelled our creed, memories of the whole pledge process came flooding in. Everything we wanted to change and improve in the fraternity seemed suddenly within reach. And as we neared the end, I think we all realized what today was. It was our initiation.

As we finished, proud that we were able to say it without skipping a beat, the brothers did nothing but demean the performance. "You could do better than that!" "That didn't sound like they even tried!" "I can't hear you!"

The comments may have hurt if it wasn't for the brevity of the time between them and the order to put our blindfolds back on. At this point they informed us that we were going to be separated and tested on our knowledge of the fraternity. I stood there silently for a few minutes, waiting to be whisked away to some unknown part of the forest. Mentally, I reviewed my Greek alphabet, facts about our founders, and anything else about our chapter the brothers might question me on. But then without having been moved even an inch, I was told to remove my blindfold.

A bit confused, I slowly undid my tie and allowed it to fall around my neck, seeing only one of the more veteran brothers in the group, RJ, seated before me on a large stone. He was keeping the fire alive, tranquilly poking the embers at its feet. Normally, he was one of the more energetic and rowdy brothers, so I didn't know what to make of his current serenity.

He remained quiet for a minute, focused mostly on the flames roaring between us. Then, glancing up at me for no more than a single moment, he asked me to simply recite the Greek alphabet and nothing more. I did as he said, but I was still perplexed by the fact that I wasn't being given the third degree.

"I'm not going to grill you; I just want you to keep this fire alive." He declared, appearing to have read my mind.

I was skeptical; the task seemed too easy for an initiation. Especially after the week we had just been through. I walked over and grabbed the long stick he was using to stoke the flames, as he in turn stood up and walked off into the woods without a word. *Maybe he went to get more wood?* I thought as I started awkwardly imitating RJ's poking motions, slowly realizing I had no idea how to keep a fire going in these windy conditions. The wind itself seemed to pick up on my ineptitude and blew harder at the flames. The once-roaring fire was practically reduced to cinders. I was able to partially save it by adding some sticks and leaves scattered on the forest floor, but the campfire was still too weak.

I began to panic thinking I may fail because I didn't know how to keep a fire alive, but at the moment the embers seemed ready to die off, RJ came back from the shadows of the woods with a bundle of large sticks under his arms. He placed a few in the makeshift fire pit, which quickly ignited and returned the inferno to its former glory. Thankfully, I maintained enough heat for them to catch.

RJ sat back down with a sigh and told me to listen to all the yelling going on in the woods. I could hear the brothers screaming at my pledge brothers from different directions in the forest. Drilling them with questions and berating them for any slow or incorrect answers. It felt unfair simply listening in and sitting next to the warm fire while they were somewhere in the forest being put through the ringer and enduring an unmerciful chill.

"Do you want to know why I'm not doing that to you?" RJ asked calmly. Before I could even ponder the question he added "because you went through enough the other day." I was a bit surprised by what he said. I would have thought him to be an old school fraternity guy who subscribed to the notion that a pledge should do what they were told during the process, but it seemed he respected my resolve during the incident with our chapter president. He explained that he felt that the choice to persist and refuse the task of degrading the memories and tragedies that the museum represented was in line with the ideals of our fraternity. As far as he was concerned, I was as ready to join as anybody.

A slight grin crossed my face. Seeing further proof that there were men in the fraternity I could truly look up to made me feel actual pride in joining the fraternity for the first time. I thanked him, but he didn't reply.

After what seemed like forever, RJ checked his phone and finally stood up, announcing it was time to go find the rest of the initiates. We made our way around the forest, pushing through the brush and following the sound of yelling. We picked up my pledge brothers one by one. Whenever we approached, the brothers would notice RJ and I making our way to them, and quickly ended whatever mental games they were playing with my fellow pledges and allowing them to leave with us as we journeyed onward to gather everyone.

It all felt like a grand adventure. Climbing up rocks, crossing the river using steppingstones, and forcing ourselves through thicket. All to bring our group back together again. After we finally regrouped, we were taken back to the fire where I had spent the majority of the night. All the brothers were there awaiting our return, and the closing ceremonies of the initiation commenced.

There were speeches and what I assumed was the typical pageantry of such an event. The night culminated with us screaming the AKΛ creed at the top of our lungs once more, marking our entry into the brotherhood. But for me, the conversation next to the fire with RJ felt like the true conclusion of my personal pledge story, and it greatly overshadowed every moment that occurred during the official ceremony.

After all was said and done, our former taskmasters gave us one more task as neophytes in the brotherhood. They stood aside, revealing our heavy stone we had painted for AKΛ weeks earlier. We were then told why there wasn't a single rock with our letters depicted on its surface that could be found at GMU; every pledge class before us had tossed their own right there, into the river behind us. And now, it was our turn to do the same.

So, we all grabbed the rock and lifted it together up to the rocky shore. Swinging it once, then twice, then a third time. Finally bringing it up and letting it fly into the stream. As the rock plunged out of sight due to the cover of night, so too closed the curtain on our pledge process.

We were so happy it was finally over. Smiling from ear to ear, we listened to the cheers from the brothers of AKΛ behind us as we took in the moment together.

Chapter 9

Wandering

The sun must have felt determined that morning. What was meant to be a day overcast with clouds during the first official weekend of the Christmas season, was disrupted when its rays broke through and seemingly scattered all of the clouds from sight in an instant. Not feeling satisfied with simply making an appearance, the sun began to make the day unseasonably warm; a sweltering sixty degrees Fahrenheit. I'm certain it must have cracked a smile as it watched me on my two-hour journey to work.

My outfit consisted of all black dress clothes that I paired with the very same purple tie I wore throughout pledging. Over everything, I proudly wore my new black North Face fleece that I rewarded myself with a few days after being initiated into the fraternity. My clothes grew hotter and hotter with each passing moment, collecting every ray of heat that shone down on me. I cursed the shuttles at Mason that didn't function on holiday weekends as sweat began to bead on my forehead, and I felt the temperature begin to rise quickly with the sun. I was only thirty minutes into my walk, and I knew this hike across Fairfax, Virginia was going to be worse than I anticipated.

I must have seemed like a mindless zombie. Chugging along, staring at the dim screen of my phone that somehow had only fifty percent power left. Noting that it would run out of power before I made it to work, I had to do something to stretch the charge. *Maybe dimming the screen further could save me some much-needed power, and allow me to still hear the directions*, I thought. It seemed worth a shot.

But after checking my phone, not even twenty minutes further into my trek, I was already at thirty-five percent power. My eyes narrowed and my mouth dropped in disbelief; what was I going to do? Well, there was only one thing I really could do. Memorize the directions.

Now, I wasn't so confident in my own memory to believe I would make it without my phone. The plan was to simply turn off my phone, walk until I forgot my next turn, and then power it back up in order to memorize my next steps. I hoped that by repeating that cycle, I'd avoid ending up stranded and unable to call for help. So, while grumbling about my circumstance, I placed my phone in my backpack and wiped the sweat off my brow. Readjusting my drawstring bag, I started off again.

Still moaning about my day, I couldn't tell what was worse. Was it this hike in the scorching heat, or how the day began, embarrassing myself and getting rejected? I shuttered and tried to shake my head to forget that unbearable recent memory. But a long walk with no distractions often forces the mind to wander through the fields you wish they would circumvent. And while I was marching under the glaring sun, hearing only the white noise of cars and wind, my mind began to do just that; meander through the memory of my dispiriting morning.

***

To a fly on the wall, my morning would have seemed normal and bland. I woke up alone in my dorm; everyone was still away for the holiday weekend, including Charles who had headed back home after dropping me off the night before. But this empty morning filled me with excitement, as I was able to convince my semester-long crush, Zee, to stop by my dorm before I left for work. She had come back to campus early after Thanksgiving and I thought this was my best chance to confess my feelings. There would be no one around to interrupt, and no need to figure out a way to get ourselves alone. Furthermore, I was still high on my new status as a brother in my fraternity, which infected me with a cockiness that I thought I'd be immune to. I took a drag of my hookah pen and hopped out of bed to get ready. I threw on my best dress clothes, the very same I adorned myself with throughout weeks of pledging, in preparation for work. The only difference to the outfit was a black shirt with our fraternity's letters, colored purple and bordered in gold, stitched into its chest that I wore underneath my ebony collared shirt out of pride.

Xavier, Zee, and I had gotten pretty close over the course of the semester. She was practically a seventh pledge brother. She often helped us with pledge tasks, came to our frat parties, and was an ever-present participant in our Special Hookah nights. Sometimes the three of us would just explore Fairfax, sharing stories and making each other laugh so hard we couldn't breathe. It got to the point where she would open up to us about her personal problems and ask for advice, and we would do the same with her in turn.

I can't remember what excuse I crafted that morning. Maybe I invited her over under the guise that I needed some of that precious advice from a woman's point of view, or maybe I said I was trying to return something she had left in the room the last time she was hanging out with Xavier and me. Whatever it was, it is lost to time. But what I do know is that for days I had been playing coy with her about having a secret crush on someone and feigning that I didn't know the best way to profess my love.

I thought I was beyond clever. Some genius Casanova playing a game of 3D chess that would end in Zee swooning into my arms from the surprise confession and begging me to skip work so she can fully enjoy the first day of a new romantic adventure. I pictured myself leaving her with only a single kiss as I departed for work.

The fantasy was so intense it left me with a dumb grin from ear to ear and practically hugging myself in the bathroom, imitating the embrace I would soon be sharing with one of the most beautiful girls on campus. A sudden knock on the door shocked me out of my fantasy, and I threw my hands to the side as if whoever was at the door could see my shameful state. I shook off my momentary embarrassment, gathered myself, and made my way to the door. Making sure to spray myself with some after-shave on the way out of the bathroom.

I opened the door and there she was. Wearing a simple, chocolate colored North Face, jeans, and Ugg boots. She couldn't have looked more gorgeous.

She said "hey girl" cheerfully as she ambled in, and I could feel a very familiar twitch in my right eye begin to pulsate; it was something that occurred every time she used that phrase with me. But this was not the time to fixate on the little things, I had to focus on the prize. I asked her how her Thanksgiving had been, hoping to spark some lighthearted conversation. After about five or so minutes I planned to bring up the subject of my mysterious crush, but it seemed Zee had other plans.

Almost immediately, she told me about some guy she had been seeing lately. Her smile was big, eyes shining brightly. As she waited for my response, she seemed giddy at the opportunity to reveal her new lover.

But there was something deeper, hidden in that smile. Something that wanted to be understood but remain unspoken. I peered deeper into her gleaming eyes, and discerned the sad, disheartening truth. Despite the grin on her face, the slight furrow of her brow gave it away. She wanted me to take a hint.

There was no hope for me ever being with her. I grit my teeth at the thought and my heart dropped. I could practically feel it falling through my body, further and further.

Past my ribcage, through my gut, and then down my leg. Until finally, it hit the floor.

Clack!

***

The sound of my phone hitting the hard sidewalk pulled me back to reality. *Great, just what I need.* I thought while picking it up, worrying that the screen was cracked. Thankfully it was fine, but I was greeted by something potentially worse. Despite my efforts, my phone was dying. With only twelve percent left, and almost another hour of my journey left to go, I began to panic. I didn't know how to get to the mall from where I was, and I was too far along to remember how to get back. Looking around I saw a shopping center just down the road. I prayed there would be an outlet outside one of the buildings that I could use and rushed over, thanking God I had brought my charger with me.

Pacing around the shopping center, I searched high and low for an outlet along the outer walls of the stores but found nothing. I knew one of the restaurants must have had an outlet for customers to use, so I rounded the shopping center once more, peering into all of the windows. I began to lose hope, not seeing a single one, until I finally found a little sandwich place. Through the glass door I could see four sockets grouped together and situated like nuggets of gold beneath a small table that stood against the wall. I stood in front of the entrance, oddly nervous to walk in. I had no desire to eat there, and for some reason I felt they could sense it. *What if they don't let me charge my phone?* I nervously pondered.

After five minutes of coming up with my perfect order to disguise my true intention, I finally made my way in. I approached the cashier and fumbled my order for a meatball sub beautifully since I was unable to take my mind off the electrical socket that would be my savior. While this would normally have embarrassed me, I was just happy she understood the message despite my stutter-filled mumbles.

Once my phone was finally plugged into the wall, I slouched back in my chair to relax. I stared at the ceiling, thinking of how that was the second time within a week I had over-thought a simple interaction...

***

"*Sigh...*Okay Drayton, moment of truth," I murmured to myself, standing outside that door on a cold autumn night.

My heart was pumping. Palms were sweaty. I went through everything that I needed to do in my head. Rehearsing again and again: *Stand up straight, be polite, don't shy away, ask questions about them.*

As Charles turned the key and pushed the knob inward, I took one last breath, preparing myself like a runner awaiting the starting gun. I readied my smile and attempted to conceal my exhaustion from the week before.

Finally, once the door was fully open and I was invited inside, it quickly became apparent that all of my prep was pointless. It didn't seem like anyone was home. I began to calm down and laugh at myself for being so nervous to meet a friend's parents, slightly embarrassed at how pensive I had been. The internal laughter swiftly became a groan as I became disappointed that I still had a long way to go. Was I a robot or something? At damn near twenty years old I should have been able to introduce myself to another human being without rehearsing.

My self-reprimand was interrupted by Charles telling me that his mother was probably upstairs laying down and that she'd be down in a few minutes. Doing all but slapping my own cheeks, I reinvigorated myself. I threw my mental script out the window and I was going to go with the flow.

Charles' mom had a very bright and warm personality. She showed me around the house and really made me feel at home. She treated me as if she had known me since I was in diapers; as if I were a visiting relative she hadn't seen in a long time. Even for someone like me, she was easy to talk to.

After she had shown me the room I'd be sleeping in, she retired back to her own for the night. Not quite feeling tired, Charles and I sat down on the couch and watched some anime that happened to be playing. I thought that was how the rest of the night was going to go, until Charles received a text.

His friends knew he was back in town for Thanksgiving, so they were all trying to meet up that night to hang out. I didn't really know them very well, but I had seen them a couple times before. In fact, these were the same friends I saw with Charles the day I met him. I had seen a few of them in passing since then, though I had forgotten most of their names; the only exception being Eunice. She was the gorgeous Latin girl that made my heart race before I even knew her name, and Charles' best friend. Thinking she may be there, I decided to go out with Charles to see his friends instead of heading to bed.

Of course, I was sorely disappointed when I didn't see her sitting amongst the rest of Charles' friends at the burger place where we decided to meet up. Not that it really mattered since I had learned from Charles that she had been dating her boyfriend for years. Normally such a fact would kill my interest, but she attracted me like a roaring campfire in the night. A beauty I could never touch. Each of the few times I had been around her during that fall semester, her glow completely outshined my crush on Zee.

Then while sitting there in the booth, listening to the group talk and reminisce, I heard them mention something. Information I didn't know how to handle. Eunice and her boyfriend had recently broken up.

My eyes widened. I felt like a bug, zipping through the skies, looking for a nice safe flower to land on. And then, out of nowhere, appeared an enticingly bright flame. It waved along with the breeze that carried its warmth, tempting me. I wanted to fly straight into the kiln right then and there.

But, I had no way of contacting Eunice on my own and I already had a pretty good friendship with Zee, so I decided it would be better to land on that sweet and familiar flower.

***

Tch...

Well, I guess I was wrong about that one huh? I thought. Turning my attention to more important matters, I looked down from the ceiling and saw my order was almost ready. I reached down to grab my phone, hoping it had the charge it needed to get me to work. I turned it back on and closed my eyes while praying to God that it would be enough; it was not.

But, based on how quickly my phone died before, it was enough to get me within fifteen minutes of the mall. I thought at that distance I should be able to see it, so making it on my own may be possible from that point. With a new determination, I picked up my sandwich, stuffed it into my bag along with my jacket and set off anew. Thanks to the short rest and removing my jacket, I felt like I had been given a second wind. With that new energy, I refused to let my morning speak for the rest of my day.

The trek became yet another challenge to conquer, and a future story I could tell my kids; complaining about how much rougher I had it as a kid and how they should be grateful that they don't have to walk two hours to work and back. At some point during the final hour of my journey, I even started to enjoy it; taking in the sights and sounds around me, such as the splashing and trickle of fountains, and the honks of geese nestled in the grass.

Sweating like a sinner in church, I arrived at my store early enough to dry off and take a load off my feet in the backroom before heading to the front counter to help at the registers. Funny enough, once I got started, I was so focused on my work that my mind was silent. A trance-like state akin to static on a tv. Thanks to that, before I knew it, my workday was already over.

At some point during that arduous Black Friday shift, I was able to secure a ride home from a coworker. The help of whom had me back in front of my dorm building before I could even doze off in her car. Once inside, I lazily walked up to my floor, placing my hookah pen in my mouth in preparation to wind down after a long day. I opened the door to my suite, and of course, there still wasn't another soul present. I walked over to Xavier and Nick's side to confirm my solitude, but then our famous, squeaky Swagger Wagon caught my eye. I took a seat in the small purple and gold wagon to have a smoke, leaning back and letting my arms and legs hang over the edges. Something about it just felt right.

I squeezed the button on my disposable vape and took a large, deep drag. Letting out a big puff of smoke, I watched the thick cloud rise upward. As it billowed against the ceiling, it made me wonder. *Will I ever get the opportunity to embrace the flame, since landing on the flower didn't pan out?*

Chapter 10

Choices

Tears streamed down my face as an inescapable pain stabbed my gut. *Please God, help me. I've learned my lesson.*

The two weeks left in the 2012 fall semester were some of the busiest days of my college life, and it all started with fraternity elections. Not too long after our initiation, we needed to participate in the vote for the executive board of our AKΛ chapter. Each one of my pledge brothers was trying to earn a position, and I was no exception. I myself sought two positions: the New Member Education and Philanthropy chairs. I wanted to bring a change to the pledge process of our chapter, and I also really believed in the cause "These Hands Don't Hurt," which was at the center of AKΛ's philanthropy efforts. I intended to lead the charge in revolutionizing our disjointed processes and bring an end to our spasmodic method for educating recruits.

But once the voting got underway, it became clear that our new member status was a source of contention amongst the brothers. Though many argued on our behalf, stating that we should be able to participate if we wanted to contribute to the organization, most of the executive board was against it. By the look of their faces, those that supported The President were clearly unhappy with our presence as well, but they remained quiet and unfazed while watching the discussion; probably aware that our participation would not be enough to threaten their power or influence within the fraternity.

Our chapter was essentially divided into two factions. One group treated AKΛ as an asset to be milked, and the other took the "social" in "social fraternity" to heart. The former being more responsible and focused on the image of AKΛ, while the latter concentrated their efforts on having fun and organizing events. Knowing that, it should surprise no one that all the brothers that had recruited the members of my class belonged to the social group. They also were the only members in support of our participation in the elections.

Of course, there were some members who tried to build a bridge between these two warring nations, such as RJ and Troy, but it seemed all for naught as the group continued to yell and argue at every turn.

What should have taken less than an hour, quickly turned into almost two. At the end of it all I somehow earned enough trust within the brotherhood to be rewarded with the New Member Education Chair, while also being given joint responsibility over philanthropy efforts along with Xavier and Trace. As our recently retired Pledge Class President, Xavier was further granted a seat on the executive board as the secretary despite his new member status; much to the chagrin of The President. Maybe it was due to his serious and organized nature, or perhaps the brothers noticed his ability to stay calm and collected under any circumstance. Who knows? All I know is that even though I hadn't gained such a high position myself, I felt just as empowered. It really began to feel like our pledge class was going to change this group for the better from top to bottom.

The next couple days were filled with me planning out the course of the next pledge process, while researching and designing potential philanthropy events. I wanted to impress the other brothers and show that it wasn't a mistake placing so much responsibility onto the new initiates. But, doing all of this in addition to my studies caused me to overextend.

Every moment of my day was filled to the brim. If I wasn't in class, I was at work. If I wasn't mapping out a curriculum for the fraternity, I was studying. Since there weren't enough hours in the day, I had no choice but to pull all-nighters; though in the long run these seemed to do more harm than good, as I rarely remembered more than a quarter of what I studied. Those meager returns on my studious investments never felt worth the trouble, but if there was a better option, I didn't know it at the time.

Final exams loomed over me like a rattle-boned desert hawk, waiting for an easy and weak meal to scurry out of its den. My stomach twisted and cramped out of hunger as I glued myself to my desk, desperately memorizing every slideshow and document our professor may test us on. I did my best to distract myself from the pain, but food became all I could think about. Telling myself it would just be a quick break, I walked over to Xavier's side of the suite. He too seemed eager for a reason to pull his nose out of the books, and we began to complain about how tired we were of the fast food on campus, and how we wished our dorm had a kitchen so Xavier could show off his skills. During the pledge process he had often made mouthwatering meals in any kitchen that he could find, but the depth of his talent was only on full display when he acted as our chef and saving grace during the night of Hell Week where we were required to make a Thanksgiving meal for the brothers.

I joked with Xavier, saying that they were lucky I was absent for the majority of that night thanks to a shift at the mall, or I probably would have mangled every dish I touched. I was the complete opposite of Xavier when it came to cooking. Practically afraid of the oven, I rarely entered the room it called home. But despite this, and knowing I couldn't cook anything else, I asserted that I could make the best grilled cheese that would ever grace Mason's campus.

For every dish I never learned to cook, I took the time to perfect the grilled cheese. The best way to get the bread perfectly toasted. The perfect amount of butter and bacon. I'd even spent many of my summer days taking random ingredients from the fridge and finding a way to add them to my recipes. Everything from the scrumptious addition of Pico de Gallo, to the soggy and less than successful attempt at adding fresh sliced strawberries. There was nothing I wouldn't try once in my venture for the perfect grilled cheese.

But alas, Xavier doubted my hyper-focused training with tomato soup's best friend, and in lieu of studying, and ignoring our new duties as brothers, we decided to hold a competition for the ages. A night of grilled cheese and gluttony.

In order to bring this culinary showdown to fruition, we'd need to recruit the fickle-natured duo of Zee and Amanda; Zee had a kitchen on the ground floor of her dorm building that was fundamental to our goal, and Amanda had a car that we could use to get supplies.

Normally, I wouldn't have imagined continuing to speak to a woman that had rejected me, purely out of shame and a fear of awkward tension hanging in the air, but this time was different. The most obvious reason being that I was rejected by Zee before I could even tell her how I felt about her, so I couldn't be too upset, but I also took petty comfort in knowing that her new relationship was an active train wreck being caused by her fickle and inconsiderate habits I was blind to before.

Against my wishes and in total disregard of my pleadings to stop, she continuously referred to Xavier and I as "girl." She also developed a habit of making us wait for hours as she figured out if she had other plans or not. Often, she would only settle for hanging out with us if the night involved Special Hookah or an invite to one of AKΛ's parties. She never treated us badly, but we were clearly not her favorite people to spend time with on a Friday night. We were more of a safety net that prevented her from slipping into boredom or loneliness on the weekends. While being her back-up friends stung, having a pretty girl around that could keep up with our quips and sense of humor always felt like a nice bonus. Not to mention girls tend to look in your direction more when you already have one standing beside you, so I can't say we didn't get anything out of the relationship.

To the surprise of no one, Zee had more exciting plans than spending time with us the night of our challenge. Amanda also had some studying to take care of for finals season, so it seemed all hope was lost. But it was then that Xavier and I remembered another option, Zipcar. Zipcar was a service that allowed you to conveniently rent a car on campus, though at what I considered exorbitant by-the-hour prices; at least on a college student's budget. Xavier didn't make much through work study and folding clothes didn't exactly leave me flush with cash, so we'd just have to rush to the store to buy our ingredients and cookware, then bring it back within an hour to pay the cheapest price possible. Piece of cake.

Then all we needed was a kitchen. We searched high and low, but everyone was too busy being responsible with their studies. With a rented car full of groceries, we couldn't give up on our quest. So, Xavier had to work some magic and convince Zee to just let us in; telling her she didn't need to stay with us and that we would make sure to leave everything how we found it so that the Resident Advisor wouldn't even question who had been using it.

Zee eventually conceded, though I imagine with an eye roll and matching sigh. Once we entered that small community kitchen, we immediately pulled out all of our assorted meats and cheeses and divided them between us. We set our chips and two cases of Capri Sun to the side, readied our pans, and fired up the stove. What followed was a beautiful symphony of sizzling meat, the clanging of spatulas against metal, and the crunch of bacon as we snacked through the entire performance. The smell of butter mixed with garlic and onion powder filled the air, quickly followed by the enticing smell of melting cheese.

As our stack of grilled cheeses grew, passersby would stick their heads in, amazed at the tower of grilled cheeses and drooling at the scent. Occasionally, Zee would come down to check on us, and at some point even Amanda stopped by in order to give us some Christmas gifts. As she handed Xavier a small box that was wrapped neatly with paper and adorned with a bow, it became apparent that the jug of milk that remained in her left hand was meant for me. I stared disconcertedly at the shiny crimson bow that was taped to its cap. I had once told her in passing that I loved milk, but this seemed silly. I couldn't help but think that sometimes the thought doesn't count, since she obviously didn't think beyond the most basic fact about me. Hell, I didn't even have a fridge in the dorm large enough to store a gallon of milk.

But, still appreciating that someone got me a gift at all and wanting to show it, I took that jug and bet everyone that I could drink it all in one go; believing my love of milk would carry me through the challenge. It did not.

Despite the cheering as I glugged down the milk, I was only able to finish about half before my experience told me one more sip of this ivory nectar would send me straight to the bathroom to vomit. Everyone feigned disappointment and we all burst out into laughter at the ridiculousness of my attempt. Seeing Amanda smile, I knew my job was done. Feeling accomplished, I returned to the kitchen with Xavier to finish what we started, tossing the remainder of the milk straight into the trash once Amanda had turned her back.

Soon after, Xavier and I sat across from each other in the common area with our grilled cheeses piled up like pancakes. The two cases of Capri Sun rested on the floor to each of our rights, ready to wash down the deliciousness that was coming, and they were each accompanied by a variety pack of chips that were intended to add some crunch to our banquet.

The cheese was perfectly gooey, oozing out the side of the golden-brown bread that contained it. The bacon bits I had made from crumbled bacon strips filled every bite, along with the faint flavors of garlic. My sandwich turned out precisely how I wanted, and I knew I'd won. Xavier knew he had also made an excellent sandwich, but reluctantly agreed that he'd been bested after sampling both of our creations multiple times. Cheesy as ever though, he exclaimed that we both won, and that "these will be the times we remember for the rest of our lives."

I agreed with a chuckle, simultaneously letting the food coma take me as I was filled with inner peace. At that moment, I could tell everything was going to be okay. Not only in classes, but in life.

Or so I thought until my stomach began to bubble, and I felt an urgency that I had never felt before. I rushed to the bathroom, throwing the door open and shutting it just as fast. Apparently milk didn't love me back anymore, and I was about to learn that lesson in the harshest way possible. As I cried out to God for relief from that unbearable agony, the experience became engraved in not only my mind, but also my body. For the good and the bad, Xavier was right. How could we ever forget a night like that?

***

Days later, At the end of finals week, Xavier ended up dating Amanda, despite being rejected when he had first popped the question a week earlier. I was skeptical of what could make her change her mind, but the joy that Xavier emitted was too pure to tarnish with suspicions.

After he told me, I snuck away to clear my head and walk through the nearly empty campus. I was happy for Xavier, I truly was, but I was slightly worried this meant the good times we were having as two pathetic bachelors were going to come to an end. Deep down I was also jealous. Why was he able to come out of the semester with the girl he wanted, but not me?

Thinking once again about Eunice, I was determined to test myself and ask her out on a date the next time I saw her. Having recently had my braces taken off, and now sporting my letters, I felt like I may have had a chance. It didn't hurt that I had finally started growing some chin hair and would be graduating from my barely-noticeable, prepubescent mustache either.

Eunice was the most intimidating woman I had ever met until that point, so even if she declined it would feel like an accomplishment. I took a resolute drag from my hookah pen, before blowing the vapors out my nose and turning around to go home.

As I walked down the sidewalk leading to my building, I noticed someone had been walking about twenty-five or so feet behind me for a while. I could barely see them just out of the corner of my eye, but it seemed like someone familiar. I looked into the reflection in the glass windows of the building next to us, hoping to catch a better glance of whoever it was. And who would have guessed, it was Amber. Since she could only see the back of my new jacket, I doubted she knew it was me. I wondered where she might be going at this time, but it didn't really concern me, and I ceased to pay it any mind. That is, until I turned the corner to head toward our building's entrance and realized she was going to the same place.

Since I knew she didn't live in our building, and therefore wouldn't have a key, I had two choices: face a potential awkward interaction and keep the door open for her, or let the door close behind me and leave her out in the cold until someone came down to get her. Option A would clearly show my growth and that I was attempting to be the bigger person about what happened between us, whereas Option B would betray a petty nature deep within me.

By the time my hand touched the door, my choice was already clear. I wish I could say I was the bigger person that day, but I wouldn't trade the petty joy I felt in those moments for the world. Looking through the crack of the closing elevator doors, I could see her frustration mounting as she stood outside in the freezing weather. I pulled out my disposable e-hookah and took a single puff. As the elevator carried me up to my floor, I let out the smoke with a chuckle, thinking, *this is why I'm single.*

Chapter 11

Dreams Come True

Blindfolded and sitting in the backseat of Amanda's car, I zealously awaited for what was to come. I attempted to heighten my sense of hearing by pure force of will, hoping to gain a clue as to where I was being led. Try as I might, the only sounds I could discern from the laughter and conversation around me were passing cars and honking horns. I could make out lights through the space between the threads, but I couldn't distinguish any shapes.

I could feel the burning stare of the vigilant sentinel, Zee, making sure I didn't peek and ruin the surprise, as Xavier led us to a secret destination via whispered directions to Amanda, who volunteered to drive for the occasion. The giggles in the car intensified as I guessed incorrectly again and again where I was being taken. I felt giddy with excitement; the mystery of it all had me on the edge of my seat. I bit down on my lips to contain my elation.

Then suddenly, I could see a bright light shining through my blindfold, and I just knew that we had arrived. Xavier told me I could remove my blindfold and I threw it off without question, peering through the blinding white lights that surrounded us. As my eyes adjusted, I was slowly able to recognize where we were.

"Surprise! We're here to get you some freaking gas!" yelled Xavier at the top of his lungs.

Confused, I was about to feign some form of appreciation before I was told not to be stupid and to put my blindfold back on. It seems Amanda was just running low on fuel, and we had to make a pit stop at a gas station that was along the route. Relieved that I wasn't getting gas for my birthday and feeling gullible for ever giving credence to the idea, I happily allowed Zee to cover my eyes once again.

About fifteen to twenty minutes later, we arrived at our true destination. I shed my blindfold slowly, revealing a huge and unfamiliar sign that read Dave & Buster's. As impressive as the huge neon orange and blue sign was, I had no idea why I should be excited for it. But much like the very first night I had smoked hookah or when I discovered the joys of a room filled with trampolines, my inner child was awakened when Xavier compared the establishment to an adult Chuck E. Cheese. With eyes shining with glee for the games and mouth-watering food inside, I almost forgot to say thank you before rushing up to the door.

Once inside, Xavier paid for the chips needed to play the games and the hostess took us to our table to eat. Upon seeing our table, my excitement was relegated to the back of my mind and superseded by a wave of emotions I couldn't pin a name to. It was as if the world went white, and all that remained was our table and my friends. But not just the friends that whisked me away to this temple of fun. Already seated at the table were Charles, John, and Caleb.

The emotions continued to flow within me when I heard everyone at the table yell "Happy Birthday!" I wasn't sure how to react. I was ecstatic, embarrassed at being the center of attention, teary eyed, but also apprehensive and scared. This seemed too good to be true. A surprise party: a night out where both my groups of friends were coming together to celebrate me. It was a queer feeling, but it was also the most heartwarming thing that had ever happened to me. This was everything I had ever wanted, so I submitted myself to the moment and enjoyed every bit of it.

Time unfroze as I darted over to hug and greet everyone that had come. I thanked Xavier unendingly for planning the entire thing. During what became known as Grilled Cheese Night, I told him that I hadn't been treated to a birthday party with friends since I was in elementary school, never expecting him to break the streak. Especially since my actual birthday had passed nearly two weeks earlier, during our winter break. If I didn't know it before, that day I was certain. Xavier was the most caring and empathetic person I had ever met. He went above and beyond for everyone he called his friend. Over the course of the previous semester, he had become my roommate, my friend, my confidant, and my pledge brother. In him, I hadn't just found a lifelong buddy; I had found my best friend.

Honestly, the rest of my birthday celebration was a whirlwind of fun that I recall more as a feeling than an actual event. I never wanted the night to end, but before I knew it the table was being cleared of plates and crumbs, and our chips had run dry. My only mementos of the occasion were a shot glass inscribed with the Dave and Buster's logo and some candy from the prize stand; both costing way more tickets than one would expect, but I would have paid any price for even the smallest physical reminder of one of the happiest moments of my life.

About a week later, I found myself at a very different kind of party, but unlike the previous, nothing about the party itself stood out. It was your typical college gathering; a house filled with too many eager lushes, and too little space. Not only that, the drive, free of blindfolds and secret destinations, was equally ordinary. Yet still, my heart pounded violently against my chest, incrementally so, as anticipation surged through my veins; this time, not only was I accompanied by Charles, Xavier, and Zee, but most importantly, Eunice who had decided to tag along.

We were in one of the back rooms of the house standing in a circle and enjoying the music. In one hand I held some vodka-soaked gummy bears, and in the other was a cup of the famous college concoction called Jungle Juice. I threw the gummy bears into the back of my throat, while washing them down with the sweet brew, as if I were taking pills of daring. Despite my efforts, it seemed as if all of my nervousness had been burning off the alcohol, because I didn't feel the spike in mettle I normally experienced after so many drinks in quick succession.

In contrast, it seemed Eunice had already started to feel the effects of her sole drink, giggling up a storm and dancing to the bass heavy tunes being played by the DJ that was stationed on the other extreme of the room. That is until she tripped over the power cord for the DJ's equipment, causing the music to abruptly stop and the lighting to shut off. As I quickly bent down to turn everything back on, the crowd's eyes turned to me as the DJ made a joke about how some of us were getting too "turnt", pointing his finger in my direction. I sheepishly plugged the cord back in, feeling ashamed for something I didn't even do as everyone in our group covered their mouths and snickered amongst themselves.

Thinking this would be the perfect time to suggest that she owes me, and that being my date to our fraternity's forthcoming bid night would be the perfect recompense, I stood back a few feet from our friends and gestured to Eunice; bidding her to come closer. As she approached and I leaned over to start speaking into her ear, I noticed the lights were out and the music had come to a swift halt for the second time. Looking down I could see Eunice had once again kicked the plug out of the socket, bringing the party to an awkward pause. Again, I leaned down to return the power that allowed the DJ to work his magic, and again I was greeted with a jab from the DJ. Though this time, the void left by the omission of song was filled by groans and the DJ yelling "come on man," as I returned the plug to its socket.

I nudged my clumsy crush back in the direction of our group who remained standing near the back wall of the room, far away from the plug that had ruined the most important moment of my night. My short-lived courage to ask out Eunice was gone, and I could barely bring myself to say a word to her. Even as she asked me to dance with her and pulled on my arm, I could barely unglue myself from the safety of the wall behind me; only stepping away from it by a few inches in order to shimmy back and forth in a sad attempt to dance. The sight of it all caused her to giggle unrelentingly. After placing her hand over her mouth to stifle her laughter, she looked at me with a sly smile, leaned over, and snatched my phone. Out of shock, I did nothing as she turned away and leaned on me, shoulder to shoulder, seemingly typing away at my screen.

I quickly deduced she must be putting her number into my phone. *She must be interested in me!* I shouted in my own head. I waited gleefully as she typed, feigning a desire to have my phone returned quickly in order to keep the flirty rapport going. When she handed my phone back to me, she kissed my cheek and rushed off to another room with Zee. I just knew I had hit the jackpot. If I had her number, I didn't have to ask her out at the party. I could wait until another day when we were in a calmer environment, where I was more comfortable. Far from the loud music that made yelling a requirement to be heard.

I looked at my phone, scrolling as quickly as I could, but unable to find "Eunice" anywhere in my contact list. I scrolled up and down the list, praying that maybe she added herself under a cute nickname. I stood there in disbelief as I realized the alcohol had truly taken its toll on her mind. The only new entry in my phone was for "57Euno125474," connected to a phone number that didn't have enough digits. I stared at my phone with wide eyes and a blank face thinking, *of course.*

Suddenly, I heard the music shut off once again. I looked up quickly, fearful that Eunice had somehow cut off the power a third time, but instead noticed familiar red and blue flashing lights brightening the otherwise shadowy room. Looking out the small window situated in the wall, I could see the lights passing by and moving out of sight.

I looked at Xavier and Charles and we had the same thought, *time to leave.* Without exchanging words, we located Zee and Eunice and signaled that it was time to leave. Zee grabbed Eunice and we pushed our way through the crowd, moving toward the front door. Being a group of underaged-minorities at a party mostly composed of fairer-skinned individuals, we didn't want to be around if any cops decided to stop by and shut it down. So, we hurried to Charles' car, thankful he decided to abstain from drinking so he could drive us back home at a moment's notice.

Once back on campus, we decided to grab some food and head back to my dorm to relax for a bit. Upon entering the room, Eunice asked which bed was mine and made herself comfortable, jumping in and concealing herself beneath the covers as if she was home. My right eye twitched out of nervousness, and I could feel myself getting sweaty as I grew anxious and confused as to what was going on. Neither my brain nor my heart could handle the stress. Out of instinct, I ran, turning away from my own bed and walking to Xavier and Nick's side of the room where everyone else was currently sitting and jamming to the music emanating from Xavier's speakers; leaving a beautiful girl alone in my bed, and happy to do so.

As soon as I entered the room, Charles asked me where she was. "In my bed, sleeping?" I questioned as I wondered aloud what she was doing now that I had turned tail. Xavier, Charles, and Zee laughed at my cowardice, and told me I "better get back in there and talk to her." Feeling the pressure of the room, I buckled and left to face the resting beauty. *It's just a conversation, nothing is going to happen. No need to worry.* I thought as I approached my bed.

Upon my return, Eunice immediately asked me to get in bed and lay next to her. Unable to retreat again, I complied nervously; lying flat as a board on my back to keep anything more from happening. She held my hand under the covers and spoke so close to my face that I ended up blushing. I wanted to kiss her, but it didn't feel right. *What do I do?* I wondered. *What if I disappoint her by doing nothing? What if this is my one and only opportunity?* Mentally panicking about the entire situation, I was at the point of jumping out of the bed and running again, but as we kept talking, something happened. Or rather, nothing.

All we did was talk. It was a fun and cute little conversation of little to no consequence where we bounced from one silly topic to the next. At one point she even suggested I create a Mega Bed by combining my bed with the one now left vacant and dusty by Bubba's winter graduation. I calmed down to the point where my entire posture had changed, and I now laid on my side with my face pointed toward hers. Eventually, Xavier and Charles made their way in, as I had never closed the door, and joined in on our conversation. My nerves had melted away and I confidently held her hand under the blanket the entire time, creating our own little innocent secret.

Eventually, the laughs started to die down, being replaced by yawns, and forced chuckles. The pauses in conversation grew longer and longer as our bodies gave in to exhaustion. Our eyes wandered between one another, searching for the unspoken agreement that we were ready to call it a night. Soon after, Charles started preparing himself to leave, and Eunice got up to do the same. I had been enjoying the simple fact her hand was resting in mine so much that I didn't notice I had wasted the perfect opportunity to ask her out. Now, it was too late.

I sat there feeling like a goofball, until Charles began patting his pockets in search of something. He then asked Xavier if he had left his keys in the other room, and they both headed over to retrieve them. There it was, my one last chance sent down from Heaven.

I walked over to Eunice, with my left hand rubbing the back of my neck nervously as my eyes darted between her and the wall, and proceeded to mumble an awkward invitation for her to join me at AKΛ's bid dinner. Her lack of response, squinting eyes, and face of confusion made it clear she didn't hear a word I had said. I took a deep breath and looked her in the eyes while my own shook as I fought my instincts to avert my gaze. I must have looked like a wreck as I finally shot out the question that had been plaguing my mind, "Would you want to be my date to my fraternity's bid night dinner?"

She seemed to ponder it for a moment, but then lit up and smiled. "Sure. Sounds like fun," she said. I only had enough time to stare back in disbelief as my lips slowly curved into a smile, before Charles and Xavier came back. We all said our goodnights, and she left with Charles, not once mentioning the date we had just agreed to. But as she turned the corner, just before moving out of sight, she gave me a subtle wink that left me beaming from ear to ear. I couldn't wipe the stupidly large grin off my face for hours. I couldn't believe it. I had a date. Me.

The next morning, Charles gave me Eunice's proper number, and I didn't hesitate to send her a message asking how she was feeling after such a wild night out. She revealed she didn't remember a single thing from the night before. I told her about our fingers intertwined beneath my covers and my nerve-racking invitation, but she didn't recall any of it. They were memories exclusive to me.

For the second time in twelve hours, I found myself staring at my phone with my eyes peeled wide and my lips pursed as if I had just sucked a lemon. Then, as a new message popped on my screen, my blank face shattered into one of hysterical joy as I found myself jumping from the euphoria. Eunice still thought a date with me sounded fun.

I could barely contain myself as I practically skipped down the sidewalk, imagining the perfect time we were going to have. This spring semester was turning out better than I could have ever expected. Everything was going so well that I couldn't be bothered to notice the dark clouds overhead as I whistled and strolled to Robinson Hall for a meeting with the other brothers of AKΛ.

Chapter 12

Nightmares Revealed

The moment I entered our usual meeting room on the first floor of Robinson Hall, my smile collapsed under the heavy weight of the tension that permeated the air. Most of the members belonging to The Exec Board, composed of our Secretary, Treasurer, Vice President, and The President, sat at a table in the front of the room, while the remaining brothers were seated randomly amongst the desks that were arranged into neat rows. As the sitting Secretary, Xavier had a seat reserved for him, but he wasn't present as I strolled past the long white table and selected a desk in the middle of the classroom. As a matter of fact, none of my pledge brothers were anywhere to be seen. I knew part of the agenda for today was dedicated to recruitment planning, so the decision to not include the rest of our class seemed peculiar.

The three people most excited for recruitment were the more outgoing and amiable members of Kappa Class:

Brian, Kyle and Caleb. Having the more typical alpha male fraternity attitude, they were all but a shoo-in for bringing in plenty of new recruits. I couldn't quite wrap my head around why they wouldn't be invited. Then, as Xavier walked in and took his seat at the head of the class, I noticed the look of dismay on his face. Something was wrong.

Once everyone had arrived, the meeting began and the reason for his grim semblance became clear. The Exec Board wanted to take away letters from half of the new initiates. Due to failed classes in the previous semester, Brian, Kyle, and Xavier were having their letters and positions stripped from them. They'd lose all privileges the letters granted to those who dawned them, and they would be reduced to neophytes once more; effectively turning my pledge brothers into second class citizens within the fraternity and leaving them with no more rights than a pledge. Once they acquired passing grades in all of their current classes, they'd be returned to full brotherhood status. That is, as long as they continued to pay their membership fees throughout the semester, of course.

Even putting aside my personal feelings and connections to my pledge brothers, I knew this was a grave mistake. We wouldn't only be tossing out our most vital members for recruitment, but we were killing morale for those that remained. Kyle was the only freshmen within our fraternity, and Brian was the most outgoing and universally loved member of our pledge class. Our chapter was shooting itself in the foot by relegating both of them to the sidelines.

Some of the brothers, including myself, argued that there was no precedent for this, and in fact, several pledges had failed classes in the past without being barred from full brotherhood. But The President simply rebutted by pointing to bylaws that hadn't been acknowledged in years. "Just because we did things wrong in the past, doesn't mean we will continue to do so." He said with full confidence. He then scanned the room before adding, "Many of our brothers lack responsibility and accountability. That's the reason our chapter is in debt and our grade point average as a whole has been slipping for some time. If we make an example of this pledge class, it will show future prospective members that academics and obligations are important, and that we are only interested in quality recruits." I stared at his smug face with contempt. He was right in theory, but what purpose would this example serve, if it destroyed any chances at having said future? Unfortunately, The President already controlled half of the fraternity, including two of the other three members comprising the executive board. With that level of influence and the bylaws supporting his argument, he would have no trouble garnering the votes necessary to get rid of the fourth that escaped his grasp.

I could only sit at my desk with my fists clenched beneath it, grinding my teeth as I watched the inevitable occur. Couldn't they see what they were doing? Our chapter was already suffering when it came to numbers. We were already about half the size of the other social fraternities on campus, and many of our brothers were graduating at the end of the spring semester. We needed active and motivated members like Kyle and Brian to reach freshmen students if we were going to have any hope of surviving in the long term.

Sadly, by the end of the meeting, the decision to strip the letters from Brian, Xavier, and Kyle's chests was carried out, and Xavier was swiftly replaced as Secretary.

***

After the meeting, everyone decided to walk over to the Johnson Center in order to grab a bite to eat. I'm not sure why Xavier and I agreed to go along with them. Neither of us had the slightest desire to be around our so-called brothers at the time; I was angry as all hell, and he was disheartened. He felt the castigation of Kappa Class was largely his fault since he had slept through the final exam for his statistics class, resulting in his failure. The day of the test, he arrived at his lecture hall at the normal class time, but was welcomed by nothing more than an empty room. Upon checking the final exam schedule, he realized he had missed the final by two hours.

"If just one more person had passed, if I had just checked the schedule the night before, maybe this wouldn't be happening," he pondered somberly.

My irritation peaked once we arrived at our table, and I watched everyone carry on chatting and chortling as if they hadn't just pulled out their own stitches right in front of the doctor. I sat with The President to my left, and Xavier to my right. I did my best to calm myself down, but I just couldn't. These weren't my friends. My friends were going to be punished using a suddenly discovered policy that only benefited the powers-that-be within the fraternity. This was supposed to be our chance to have a positive impact within this organization, and make it shine once again. But no more.

All I could see in AKΛ's future was doom and destruction that would crush our pledge class beneath the rubble. And as they laughed and howled as if the meeting had never occurred, I could feel blood rush to my face. All I could see was red.

Surprising no one more than myself, I slammed my palm on the table and yelled at the top of my lungs, "What the hell is wrong with all of you?" I stood up abruptly, causing my chair to slide back with a loud screech. "What is so damn funny?"

I was furious at every single one of the brothers sitting before me. I shot off, letting out a barrage of criticisms and expletives that left not only our fraternity in a dead silence as they listened, but several of the surrounding tables. I pointed at each member of our group, one by one, as I explained the hypocrisy of their decision to punish our pledge class but continue to let their older members drag AKΛ further into the mud without consequence. I screamed about their failures to live up to the AKΛ creed, and I voiced every gripe and grievance I had with the brothers among me. Only one member escaped my wrath, RJ, as I made my way around the table. Finally, I reached the man sitting next to me, The President himself. As far as I was concerned he was the worst one of the bunch. "How do you let any of this go on under your watch? You're leading this fraternity to its end. You should be ashamed." I spit out, heaving as I struggled to catch my breath after my tirade.

"Watch it, Anthony," our esteemed president warned. "Or what?" I retorted sarcastically, turning my body in his direction and glowering back at his irate visage. Suddenly he stood up, his chair thrown back by the force and slamming against the linoleum floor. He flew towards me, but I remained frozen in place. Time slowed down to a crawl as I witnessed The President lunge at me; his violent intentions reflected in his eyes. I was baffled at the idea that The President of our organization would be so quick to start a physical altercation in the most public place on campus. Befuddlement and fear of his hulking build took hold of my body and left me frozen in place with my arms at my side. I mentally prepared myself for an impact that would send me crashing to the floor like the chairs we had abandoned.

Then out of the corner of my eye, I noticed two arms zip past me just before our muscle-bound leader had reached my face; pushing him back and causing him to stumble. It was Xavier. Time sped back up, and The President jutted forward once more, grabbing Xavier's throat. The brothers behind The President stood up and placed their arms around him trying to pull him back; my hands in the meantime were attempting to pry our president's from around Xavier's neck.

Within seconds we were able to pull them apart, but the damage had been done. AKΛ had dug its own grave and, in due time, it would lay in it. Tears of anger streamed down Xavier's face as he screamed curses toward everyone standing in front of him. Xavier and I stormed off to our dorm, followed by a young woman who called for our attention. Claiming to have witnessed everything, she gave Xavier a card for a lawyer in case anything were to happen. What I now realize was an opportunist, at the time, I viewed as irrefutable proof that we were the victims. Feeling that much more justified, we told our pledge brothers what had happened through text, and Kyle joined us in our decision to leave the fraternity.

Once back in the room, my ire continued to burn and I updated my Facebook status, expressing my disgust at the whole childish situation. Almost as quickly as the status was uploaded, I received a message from Josh, one of the brothers that was very close to The President. Clumsily, he attempted to walk a diplomatic slack rope. While saying things like "I'm not defending The President" and "I expect more from the head of our brotherhood too," he also excused The President's behavior by saying "he acts the way he does because he cares deeply for the fraternity," and placing the majority of the blame on the grades of our three failing pledge brothers; he saw fit to remind me that he was one of the brothers that had stressed the importance of grades the most. He even went as far as to echo the same vile intent of The President: "We wanted to make an example of your pledge class."

My mouth was left agape at his replies. Unable to deal with the situation any longer, I allowed Xavier to take over the chat. Since he was the one physically assaulted, he was understandably more furious than I.

"Brothers do not put their hands on other brothers," he exclaimed. "How could anyone stand to wear the same letters as such a brute. A president should be the best among us and know how to control his emotions." Before finishing the conversation, Xavier declared his unofficial resignation from the organization.

I was about to do the same, but my fingers paused as I remembered my date with Eunice. Without the fraternity, I wasn't sure I even had a date. Thinking about it further, I would probably lose my easy access to all future parties on campus as well. Then I thought about all of the fraternal activities and leadership positions that would look great on my resume. Caleb, Trace, and Brian, who seemed likely to remain in the fraternity even if we left, also came to mind. I thought about Nick, our roommate, and the other brothers such as Ray or RJ in the fraternity who loved AKΛ more than anything and carried themselves like true stand-up men. I didn't want to lose any of them. I felt trapped. Forced to make an impossible choice. I knew if I remained a member of AKΛ my heart would no longer be in the organization, as the ambition that set me on the path of reforming this group was shattered the moment The President's hands touched my brother Xavier.

***

Later that day, feeling the need to escape anything even remotely related to the fraternity, I made my way to Charles' building to play board games with him, John, Ayush, and Charles' suitemates. During pledging, I often snuck away a few times a week to join them in one of their daily games. A wild game of "Risk" here, a nerdy session of "Yu-Gi-Oh!" there, and often a few rounds of "Flux" and its ever-changing rules in between. Each game was a momentary reprieve from the stresses of pledging and allowed me the chance to decompress. That day was no different.

I recounted the acrimonious events of that morning to everyone. Charles' eyes widened; silently yelling *what have you gotten yourself into?* A monotone and elongated "wow" slipped out of John as his jaw dropped. Everyone seemed to share the opinion that I should leave the fraternity. Well, all but one. As per usual, Charles didn't have much to say on the topic of the fraternity itself, but he concurred that it must be hard to give your all when your best friend has been wronged and physically attacked. "I'd just wait to see how everything goes on your date with Eunice," he suggested. "Things will probably calm down by then and you can decide what to do with a cool head." I saw no holes in his logic. In fact, I thought following it would allow me to have my cake and eat it too.

As the days leading up to the bid night dinner rolled by, I prayed that he was right and that eventually the storm in my spirit would die out. But it never did. With each passing day, I felt increasingly uneasy about going to a dinner meant to celebrate the next generation of AKΛ brothers. I couldn't forgive the complacency within the organization, and the enabling of those abusing their power. The thought of bringing more unsuspecting fools into that chaotic ouroboros made my skin crawl, so I avoided all but one rush event they hosted.

In line with the status quo, the events held by AKΛ during Rush Week were disorganized beyond belief. Some so poorly planned that many brothers didn't know what time to show up. Unlike our resident freshmen Kyle, who refused to aid the cause and walked the same path of retraction as Xavier, Brian took it upon himself to attend every single rush event, despite having his letters removed. Unfortunately for our chapter, the presence of his bright and "bro-ish" personality couldn't compensate for the absence of others that could match his energy; who would want to join a fraternity that could barely scrape together five members at a time?

There was only a single glimmer of hope that week. It was a game night set up by one of my favorites amongst the brothers, Ray, that was held at the Best Buy where he worked. The brothers were present in full force, including myself, and the back area of the store was filled with prospective members playing video games on televisions larger than anything that could ever fit into a dorm. But even after such a promising night, nearly none of our guests were seen ever again.

I would be lying if I said it didn't make me chuckle when I found out that we only had three new recruits; only three guests of honor that would be present at the bid night dinner. It was a joke. Exactly what I felt our fraternity deserved.

The night of the bid dinner, I laughed with Xavier at the fraternity's expense as we got ourselves ready for the pathetic soiree, slowly realizing I had become a brother of AKΛ in name alone. I wore a simple gray collared shirt with my purple pledge tie and some black slacks. Over my shirt I wore my new North Face proudly, with three of my disposable hookah pens resting inside the inner breast pocket. Dressed to the nines, I was solely focused on creating the perfect date, and of course, I had everything planned out to ensure it went exactly how I imagined.

I had convinced Xavier and Amanda to join Eunice and me that night, for which I was completely over the moon.

They were the most crucial factor. Without them, between my nerves and being seated among those I felt estranged to, going on the date and expecting anything but failure seemed foolhardy. A double date was sure to help keep my anxiety at bay, and Amanda taking care of transportation removed the burden of securing a ride.

But man makes plans and God laughs, so throughout the remainder of the night I would watch in horror as my scheme received blow after blow that left it sprawled on the ground, bloody and beaten.

***

I knew as soon as Xavier started to have trouble contacting Amanda an hour before our meet up time, 6:00pm, that things were going to go poorly. It was like watching a self-fulfilling prophecy written by my strong belief in Murphy's Law unfold. I had already smoked through two of my hookah pens in a panic, when Amanda finally walked through the door; fifteen minutes before we were supposed to be picking up Eunice from the McDonald's across the street from George Mason's campus.

Amanda was drenched in sweat and carrying her gym bag. *Maybe she lost track of time.* I thought, attempting to quell my frustrations. But when Xavier asked if she had seen his calls and messages, she nonchalantly informed us that yes she had, but about an hour earlier she got the urge to exercise and get in a good sweat at the gym. She was well aware of the time, but couldn't bring herself to skip the workout. "I got back before it was time to leave, so it's okay." She asserted as she made her way to our shower.

I swiveled my head to Xavier as she closed the shower door, my eyes screaming. The frustration and guilt in his eyes were clear as he silently asked for forgiveness.

I didn't have the benefit of time since our ride was currently showering off her gym funk, so I made the quick decision to leave and go meet with Eunice on my own. That way I could wait with her until Xavier and our tardy chauffeur had finished getting ready. Seeing only ten minutes left on the clock before 6:00pm, I relayed my plan to Xavier as I bolted out the door. There was no way I was going to leave a girl like Eunice waiting.

I was thankful for the frigid wind blowing against my face as I ran at full speed. There was no need to worry about sweating through my clothes, nor smelling like I was the one who had gone to the gym just before a night of romance. I only slowed my pace once I had crossed Braddock Road, which ran between George Mason University and University Mall where the McDonald's was located, stopping just around the corner from the entrance of the restaurant so I could catch my breath. With still a minute left until 6:00pm, I took a quick puff of my e-hookah in order to collect myself before heading inside.

There she was. Sitting at a table in the middle of the room, looking as gorgeous and intimidating as ever. She noticed me almost immediately, greeting me with a wave and a smile that I returned in the coolest manner I could muster. *You're in control, you've got this.* I sang in my head as a mantra. Then Eunice stood and collected her belongings that had been laying on the table, and I was forced to stop my wave in order to gesture to her that she should sit back down. I shook my head from side to side, clearly miffed, as I sat down with her and explained the situation. In turn, she graced me with a soft smile and expressed that she didn't mind a little wait. Her casual aura allowed me to relax and assured me that everything would be smooth sailing from then on.

Sadly, as time passed by, her once bright expression dulled and transformed into one of confusion and growing impatience. Who could blame her? Especially after Xavier showed up an hour after me, only to give us the same gesture I had given Eunice earlier, though with a much more irked demeanor. He sat down and gave us an update on what was happening, which only served to make me more anxious and increase my disdain for Amanda. Apparently, she had taken quite the long shower with no care in the world for time. To make matters worse, she forgot a specific bra she wanted to wear that night at her own dorm and forced Xavier to fetch it for her. Even after she had the bra in her hands, she somehow took so much time that Xavier became fed up and walked to the McDonald's to wait alongside us.

It wasn't until the second hand had rounded the clock forty more times, that Amanda finally arrived, and we were able to pack ourselves into her car and head to the Cheesecake Factory for the bid night dinner. During the ride, I did everything I could to portray myself as a charismatic "frat bro" and bring back the excitement for our group outing that had been dampened by the prolonged delay. I related tales of Xavier and I's drunken escapades during pledging and showed off my e-hookah to Eunice as if she had never seen someone smoke before, but all of my efforts seemed to be undermined by every literal turn made by our designated driver, Amanda. Her driving skills were so lacking, that somehow we ended up on the wrong side of the road, causing Eunice to text me about it out of fear for her life. Thankfully, there were no other cars on the street at that moment, and we made it back to the correct lane without suffering an accident.

Once we arrived at the Cheesecake Factory, the party we were joining could be seen near the entrance standing at the hostess' podium. *Maybe the restaurant had been so busy that they had to wait all this time.* I foolishly thought. *Maybe everyone else was late too.* Then, my hopes were dashed right from under my feet as Nick revealed to me that everyone was heading out to the after party. The dinner was over.

What did I expect? We were two hours late so of course they were leaving. After some quick discussion amongst ourselves, our group of four decided to grab our own table. Based on how the night was going, it seemed like a better idea to stay put and eat, rather than get back in the car and risk further disappointment.

Little did I know, nothing could save that night. I was spiraling in my own mind; unable to pull myself out of my own head and live in the moment after so many strikes to my perfect plan. I became unable to maintain a proper conversation, especially as Eunice's face continuously divulged more and more of her boredom. Even the after party that should have been our saving grace was winding down to a close once we arrived. Distraught, I decided to call it quits before I fell behind any further. I asked one of the brothers,

Josh, to take us back to GMU instead of riding back with
Amanda; the least I could do after nearly boring her to death
was make her feel safe during the trip home.

While he drove us back he was genial and inquisitive,
asking how we met and how our night had been going. While
we filled him in on all the details, I had a momentary spur of
bravery and placed my hand on Eunice's. I wanted to know
everything was still okay after such a terrible night. I wanted
to know I'd have another chance to show we'd be great
together. To my surprise, she flipped her hand and held mine
as she smiled and leaned against me. That was all I needed to
melt away all of my worries.

As Josh dropped us off in front of my dorm, Charles
had also pulled up and parked a few spots away to pick up
Eunice. We hopped out of Josh's car, wished him a safe night
on the road, and waved him off. And there we were. Standing
in front of one another waiting for the other to speak.

This is your moment Anthony. I thought as I went in to
hug her and ask her out on another, hopefully better, date. But
as I reached in, she took a slight step back and looked down
pensively. Looking up slowly and peering gently into my eyes,
she told me she wasn't ready to start dating again. She did her
best to assure me that the events of the night had nothing to
do with her feelings; that I was a very nice and fun guy to be
around. Yet not a single fiber in my confused body believed
her, and I cursed my lame existence.

She must have seen the dejection on my face, since she
then pulled me in and kissed me on my forehead before
saying she'd be happy to hang out again as friends. I was

bewildered even further by the gesture, but waved her goodbye with the best smile I could muster as she walked off and stepped into Charles' car.

I dragged my feet back to my dorm; a feeling of desiderium filled my heart. Only the mesmerizing site of the rising vapor I released from my lungs every time I took a drag from my disposable hookah brought me any relief.

Once I was sat at my desk, and without any distraction, pessimistic questions and thoughts filled my head like a bucket under torrential rain: **"You're too damn quiet."** **"You deserve this for scoffing at your fraternity."** **"What is wrong with you?"** **"You'll probably die alone."**

But, while drowning in my thoughts, one notion pulled me down further into dread faster than the rest. **"You're so damn pathetic that she had to give you a kiss so she wouldn't feel bad."**

That same cynical idea reverberated through my head until finally a single tear rolled down my cheek and I slammed my head on my desk, hitting the spot on my forehead where Eunice had kissed me. Again and again, I slammed the dead center of my forehead against my desk, trying to silence the thoughts in vain. In the end, with my forehead swollen and unable to endure any more punishment, I looked up to the ceiling and cried.

Eventually Xavier had returned to our suite and came over to my room to see how the rest of my date went. One look at my depressing state told him everything he needed to know. He went back to his room and brought back our famous Special Hookah and some booze we had laying around the dorm. We drank and we smoked for the rest of the night. He listened to my woes, encouraged me to push forward, and helped to calm my mind as much as he could. I guzzled down every drop of alcohol I could and smoked until my throat felt scorched by the warm vapors; all to forget the issues I had been facing. From difficulties in classes, to my date that night, everything was pushed back to the recesses of my mind. For just a few hours, I simply enjoyed the camaraderie that Xavier offered in spades. The night ended with me in my newly constructed Mega Bed; intoxicated and happy to just have a friend like Xavier to lean on. Before I knew it, I fell asleep still wearing all of my clothes, albeit disheveled and smelling of spilled drink.

That night I dreamt of Eunice. She was in the Johnson Center getting help while registering for classes. She was wearing a beautiful knee-length purple dress that seemed to emit its own glimmering light. I went over to see how she was doing, hesitating for a moment as I approached her from behind. I could sense something familiar. Something sinister.

Before I could form a single theory as to what I was feeling, Eunice turned around and brandished a smile that had frequented my dreams for years. A sly smile that was just large enough to reveal the fangs behind her lips. I looked down to see my shadow expanding as it pulled me downward. I looked back at Eunice, only to see those sharp teeth held in a mischievous smirk. The darkness covered my eyes and then dispersed, seemingly immediately. As I expected, I was back in the all-familiar cave with the same witch standing upon the same rocky slope. I dreaded more than anything, the part that came next.

She raised her hands, the usual smoke trails emerged, and she slowly walked down the long, steep crag. She asked me the same inaudible question that she always did; easily identifiable by the chills it sent down my spine and trepidation it shot through my soul. The fear, as always, shocked me awake and left me stewing in sweat and gasping for air upon opening my eyes.

My head felt like someone had been smacking me around all night. I walked over to the sink to get some water, cupping the nectar of life in my hands and taking a sip. I cupped some more and splashed it on my face, letting the water run down my face and neck as I stared into the mirror. Remembering my disastrous night, my only thought was, *what now?*

***

I'd soon find out the answer was simply more of the same. I tried turning the other cheek, putting aside my own feelings for The President and his regime, but my passion never returned. Even as I put all of my effort into the duties of my elected positions, I could never quite get my heart back into it. Not only because two of my pledge brothers had effectively left the organization, but because I felt I was constantly surrounded by indolence. Whether it was educating the new members, or setting up philanthropy events around campus, I was constantly disheartened by many of my fellow members and their lack of participation in anything that didn't involve carousing. I still remember the long morning I had spent painting the windows of one of the campus burger joints. They were hosting our fundraiser for These Hands Don't Hurt, and our star pledge, Garrett, was the sole person to come to my aid. Not a single brother showed up until it was time to cavort and attract patrons to the restaurant, despite most offering their help to decorate days earlier.

Even when it came to dating, all I encountered was more disappointment. Charles had told me, a few days after our horrendous outing, that Eunice still thought I was cute, and that there was nothing I had done wrong; the date just hadn't felt right to her. Simple-minded as I was and desperate for love, I interpreted this as her needing more time before she could accept her feelings for me. Later, I found out Eunice had started seeing someone else over the course of the season, and I gave up on dating altogether for the rest of the semester. In its stead, I turned to the sweet love of the bottle and Special Hookah.

By the time classes were over, and it was time to move out of the dorms, I was physically, spiritually, and mentally drained. After an exhausting week of final exams and all-nighters powered by coffee, chain smoking hookah pens, and mystery energy pills I bought off of a brother in the fraternity, I wanted nothing more than to go home and take advantage of some R&R.

A few hours into the ride back to South Carolina, noting my exhaustion and feeling too fatigued to finish the drive home himself, my dad stopped at a hotel, and we reserved a room for the night. As we stepped into the space and laid our bags on the floor, my legs went weak, and my mind became fuzzy. I felt myself losing control of my body; only having enough energy to squeak out the phrase "Dad, I don't feel good" as I started to fall back, and my vision darkened. My dad grabbed me and lowered me onto the bed. I watched him through the shadowy haze as he grabbed me some water. He sat me up slightly and helped me sip from the tiny paper cup, lovingly monitoring my expressions and every faint motion I made. "Relax," he commanded, "you're going to be okay."

Chapter 13

Downhill Fast

Another August, another drive up to Mason with my dad, contemplating what was to come. Despite the disaster that was the second half of my sophomore year, I was optimistic and ecstatic to return to campus. With nowhere left to go but up, I was free of any concerns at the start of my junior year. Especially since I was kicking off a new semester by driving my golden 2003 Toyota Camry up to Mason. Finally, I would be rid of my dreadfully long commutes on Mason's buses, and having my own ride couldn't hurt on the dating front either.

Regrettably, my connection to my fraternity still felt weak and strained at best. After Xavier and Kyle had finalized the process of ending their membership in ΑΚΛ, the organization slowly began to feel like just another job; another block I could use to build my resume. I kept close ties with Trace, Caleb, and Brian, but the other brothers felt like distant associates. Due to a feeling of responsibility, I still intended to fulfill my duties as the New Member Education Chair and newly appointed Scholarship Chair to the height of my ability, but my enthusiasm for the roles was on life support. Masking my indifference would be quite the challenge, but just because I had a bad experience with the fraternity didn't mean I had the right to force my feelings on to new pledges. I could only hope that, thanks to the graduation of so many older members in May, the fraternity could finally be saved by the clean, young blood.

For another year I'd be sharing a suite with Xavier and Nick, and, just like last year, fate was the arbiter of my roommate assignment. This time, the man it chose was named Trey. He seemed nice; at least based on the pictures that Xavier had sent me over Facebook. He was another young black man, and just like Bubba he was a super-senior in his final semester. Oddly enough, something about this randomly selected roommate seemed familiar, though I couldn't put my finger on why. Maybe I could have figured it out if I hadn't been so distracted by all of the likes and comments garnered by my recently uploaded photo from my family's Bahamian vacation.

Even though my dad and I took turns at the wheel, I was still exhausted by the time we rolled onto George Mason's campus and parked in front of my new dorm building on the southeast border of campus: Potomac Heights. I only drove for about half of the eight-hour journey, but it was still far longer than I had ever driven before. It didn't help that at one point my dad took an hour-long nap that left me on edge for its entire duration.

As per usual, my father helped to bring all my belongings into the new suite, unit 422, moving as quickly as possible and hoping he could be back on the road within the hour. Trey and I were assigned room B, which was located to the right of the front door when entering the dorm. On our first trip up, I went inside the room and noticed that it was empty. It appeared I was blessed with the wondrous benefit of choice; a perk of arriving on campus early I supposed. My father and I placed all of my suitcases on the bed closest to the door, and I dumped my backpack at the desk sitting in front of it.

Once everything was moved up to the room, we both agreed that we deserved a short break before heading back out onto the road and picking up a rental car for my dad's return home. I shut the door and sat on the one bulky and uncomfortable couch provided by Mason in the living room, taking it all in. The dorm felt like a palace in comparison to our last; near the door there was a large, full kitchen bordered with a peninsula that separated it from the spacious and furnished living room whose back wall contained a large window along its length. From my seat, I could also see that Xavier and Nick's room had its own bathroom that seemed identical to the one in room B.

The moment I had finished scanning the room, Xavier walked in with a couple suitcases in tow, and we simultaneously yelled "Aye!" as I shot up from the couch and we dapped into a one-armed hug. I grumbled about his bad timing since my dad and I were heading out for the car rental shop, but he countered with a wink and asserted his timing was perfect. Apparently most of his belongings were being held in a storage unit a few miles away, and my car was exactly what he needed to transport it all.

***

After dropping off my dad and watching him embark on his yearly homeward bound quest, Xavier and I drove over to the storage unit and caught up on the summer's events as we packed my car with boxes. During our talk, I invited Xavier to a party that AKΛ was hosting the following weekend in order to attract freshmen to the brotherhood. It would be held at a large house belonging to an alumni of our fraternity named Marty. Our pledge brother Trace would also be living there this semester, so the home was being postulated as the unofficial AKΛ party-house amongst the brothers.

Xavier still became heated at the very mention of the fraternity, but to my surprise, he didn't require much convincing. He admitted he was actually looking forward to the bacchanal after a lusterless summer and months of sobriety. It was time to let loose.

I couldn't have agreed more, so on the way back to our dorm I stopped and picked out a cheap and flavorless version of my usual hookah pens at a gas station. I hadn't filled my lungs with any form of nicotine in months, so I looked forward to laying back and smoking it in my room after we had carried Xavier's things inside.

But my plan was delayed when we entered our suite with our first haul of boxes, and I noticed the door to my room was ajar. While I wasn't particularly excited to meet Trey, I was ready to bite the bullet and introduce myself to my new

roommate so we could get the pleasantries over with. I
walked over and knocked on the door as I pushed it to widen
the gap, finally poking my head through when there was
enough space. But what I saw wasn't my roommate. No,
standing in front of me next to the desk on the far side of the
room was none other than Amber. I was left almost aghast in
the threshold of the door as she looked over and took notice
of my presence. The awkward silence must have lasted only a
single second before a figure rose up from behind her with its
arm raised to greet me. "Hey man, name's Trey! You must be
Anthony?" he exclaimed in a lively, yet reposeful voice,
instantly breaking the short-lived stillness. "Oh yeah, nice to
meet you" I stammered out as I switched my attention to him
and shook his approaching hand.

Trey was a slim man that was about an inch taller and
a bit more muscular than myself. He wore a short goatee and
a thin mustache that he kept trimmed and neat to match his
short black hair. It felt like looking at a mirror of the future. A
future where I could finally grow more facial hair than the
stubble that currently adorned my chin.

After our brief handshake he introduced me to his
girlfriend, Amber. When my eyes met hers, it was as if a silent
pact had been made; we agreed to pretend not to know one
another. We only gave each other a lazy wave and a cold "nice
to meet you." Thankfully, we avoided any further interaction
since they were already on their way out. As Trey escorted
Amber out the main door, he said he couldn't wait to talk
more later. I gave him a nod and yelled "me neither man!" as
the door swung shut behind the couple.

The second the door to our suite closed, I couldn't help but rush over to Xavier's room to tell him what happened. I could barely contain the bellow of laughter that tried to force its way out as I ran over. The very thought of the situation made me want to laugh until my stomach hurt. My diaphragm convulsed with each suppressed chuckle. I felt like I was in a sitcom. My random roommate turned out to be my ex-girlfriend's current boyfriend. *What are the chances?* I pondered, fully appreciating this twist of fate.

I chuckled between breaths while wearing a huge grin as I told Xavier everything. But he seemed confused. "That doesn't feel awkward to you?" he inquired while furrowing his brow and staring at me sideways. "What if she comes around all the time?" he added.

I paused for a moment and mulled over the notion. All that escaped my lips was a simple "nope," followed by a slight smirk. "It wouldn't bother me at all. It's just too serendipitous to be upsetting I guess." I remarked.

Xavier tittered and a gentle grin crossed his face. "Guess it's a good thing it doesn't concern you. Nothing you could do about it now." he laughed while pointing out the obvious. "Let's just hope he thinks it's funny too if she decides to tell him."

***

Seven days later, after a week of syllabus readings, Xavier and I were having a light-hearted conversation in his room as we got ourselves ready for the party. Then a light but familiar knock at the door interrupted our conversation. "Looks like she's here" Xavier observed while walking over to

the front door and letting our visitor in. It was Amanda;
Xavier's girlfriend and our new floormate. Living so close to
her boyfriend seemed to always have her in quite the giddy
mood, and she gave Xavier a loving kiss as he wrapped his
arms around her and held her tightly. After looking up from
their smooch, she turned to me and greeted me with a hug.

I hate you. I internally proclaimed while smiling
outwardly and reciprocating the friendly embrace; feeling a
twitch in my eye. The acrimonious thought had become
automatic after last semester's disastrous double date with
Eunice. Amanda had such a large hand in what went wrong,
that I had mentally turned her into a scapegoat. Her mere
presence was enough to spark my new cognitive reflex.

Today, as per usual, Amanda would be our designated
driver to and from the party. I refused to go to my first party
of the semester and stay sober, so I was willing to leave my
car and take the chance of ending up in the wrong lane again.
Hopefully, if anything went wrong, I'd be too intoxicated to
notice.

AKΛ parties were typically composed of the same
twenty people, and Xavier and I expected no difference here.
But upon opening the door to Marty's two-story home it
became quite apparent the party was completely packed. In
stark contrast to the rest of this serene and noiseless
neighborhood situated right in front of an elementary school,
the house was full of drunk college freshmen enjoying their
first bit of true freedom away from home. It was a pleasant
surprise to say the least. To the right was a set of three steps
that led to a darkened basement-like area that had been

transformed into a large dance floor. In the corner of the room was DJ Ray, who was visible through the passageway thanks to the lights at his station. To my left appeared to be the living room where the bar could be found, surrounded by a gaggle of partygoers clamoring for more booze.

Standing near the door to the house I could see beautiful, unfamiliar girls filling the dance floor as 2 Chainz blared through the house. The fumes of alcohol and smoke filled the air despite smokers being restricted to the back patio. The scene was missing only one thing. An old friend I hadn't seen all summer. Oh, how I had missed him.

I reached into my pocket and pulled out a new disposable hookah, the very same we had picked up at the gas station a week ago. I placed it between my lips and took a nice, long drag. The green light at the tip lit up, allowing the vapor to fill my lungs until every inch was saturated. I held my breath in order to savor the subtle high it provided, finally blowing out the white haze when the temptation to see it rise to the ceiling peaked.

Satisfied, I placed the vape back into my pocket. We all then followed Xavier to the bar as he pushed through the crowd in front. It was time to down as much liquid courage as we could. After we took our first shots at the table, Xavier and I spent most of our time drinking and sitting on the sofas that lined the walls of the makeshift dance floor, occasionally getting up to dance among our own little group of three. Eventually, I was drunk enough to make awkward attempts at flirting with the entrancing freshmen girls. Somehow, surprising even myself, I charmed one of them into dancing with me for a single song. I felt like I was on top of the world after the dance was over; like maybe I did have some charisma after all. Not keen on finding out if it was a fluke or not though, I dragged Xavier outside to ride out the high of success.

We drunkenly stumbled out and away from the house and down the road; cups in hand and taking turns with the hookah pen that I had abused all night. As we traced our smoke trails upward, we couldn't help but notice how bright the night sky was. For whatever reason, we couldn't resist its call. We laid out next to each other, staring into that starry sky, right in the middle of the road that passed directly in front of the elementary school. Our cups full of drink rested on the ground next to our hands. It was a nice relief from the elation of the party. Between alcohol scented burps, we chatted about Trey and what effect his presence would bring to the dorm, what we would do on our closely approaching twenty-first birthdays, and, of course, about our love lives. I found it odd that Xavier sounded a bit distant when we made it to the subject of dating, so I asked him if he and Amanda were doing okay.

He hesitated for a moment, tapping his fingers on his belly and seemingly searching for the correct words to illustrate his feelings. After about a minute, he slowly started to open his mouth to respond, but before he could get out a single word his answer was interrupted by the cries of Garrett.

Garrett, one of our two initiates from the spring semester, jogged up to us with a worried expression and waving his arms in the air. Being his usual responsible and squirrelly self, he stopped near the top of our heads and begged us to move from the middle of the road. "What if someone calls the police? What if you get run over? You can't do this next to a school!" he asserted and questioned. We looked up at him and then at one another; a mischievous grin crossed our faces. I stood up and asked him to hold my cup apologetically and Xavier did the same.

Once both cups were in his hands and he was powerless to stop us, we mockingly declared "A pledge can't tell us what to do!" to the newly appointed brother, and dropped to the asphalt like ragdolls. Out of defiance, we started to turn and tumble down the black and gravely road. We bowled toward the end of the block with Garrett pursuing us in a panic; our laughter ringing through the quiet neighborhood like a bell tolling to the start of a new school year.

Chapter 14

Shifting Focus

Even with such an amazing start to the school year for the Beta Chi chapter of AKΛ, the road ahead was full of bumps, potholes, and blockades. Between our issues of debt stemming from unpaid dues of derelict brothers, and narrowly avoiding the shutdown of our chapter by the national headquarters of AKΛ for nearly missing a mandatory conference, we were lucky our little band of brothers was still alive. Our bureaucratic issues aside, dwindling numbers left our chapter on life support, and we all knew it. Sure, we had our new golden goose, Garrett, taking charge and putting in work for AKΛ at every opportunity, but we couldn't survive off one amazing brother. Garrett's pledge class had only two members and we couldn't have that happen again. We needed a record-breaking recruitment season if we were going to live to see another year.

With that in mind, everyone dove into recruitment with all cylinders fired. Myself unincluded, of course. With our two most charismatic and excitable brothers at the helm, Brian and Nick, I felt my unenthusiastic presence wouldn't be helpful or needed. So instead, I laid low during all of Rush Week, only attending the bid night celebration on the final evening so I could introduce myself to what I was sure would be a plethora of potential new pledges that would be taking my new member course.

But upon arriving at the bid night dinner, I would learn that excellent parties and charismatic members spearheading social efforts couldn't undo a soured and stale campus reputation. We were only able to acquire two bland and unremarkable pledges. Speaking to them made it clear they weren't fraternity material; the words unfocused, undriven, and inept came to mind. *But maybe this is exactly what AKΛ needs?* I considered. Someone that could be molded through the pledge process into a true leader that could take hold of our group that was falling apart at the seams; a shining example for how the education process of our organization can make the best of any man.

Yet, during every one of our weekly new member classes that followed, they seemed to go out of their way to prove me wrong. Constantly inquiring about future parties, asking questions with obvious answers, failing basic AKΛ history tests, and carrying themselves in such a weak and pathetic manner that the word "weeny" became added to the list of descriptors for these pitiful postulants. I felt like I was teaching a class full of five-year-olds that were pretending to be college students. The fact that they were the only freshmen interested in our fraternity seemed to foretell what was to come.

To this day, I remember the "weeniest" of the two asking me "Pwetty Pwease?" as he begged me to lend him the Swagger Wagon after I had informed them about the same rock task we had all been through as pledges. Stunned and annoyed by the cutesy tone he took with me, I stared at him silently and shook my head to say no; leaving the lecture room where I held the class without a word. My hope was that he would think to take this process more seriously and request the wagon in a more dignified manner.

Unfortunately, that was not what occurred. Instead, what followed would bring AKΛ to its knees; the damage so great that despite all the efforts made by the group of brothers, our Beta Chi chapter would never recover. Our chapter would be torn down and replaced like an old, condemned house. The address posted out front would be the same, but a new home would be left standing over the plot of land.

The next brotherhood meeting I attended we were all informed that our chapter was being investigated for hazing and that we were being suspended from engaging in any fraternal business on campus. Campus events, fundraisers, everything you could think of was now forbidden to us. I knew immediately it had to do with Mr. Pwetty Pwease.

Due to the severity of the accusations at hand, AKΛ National Headquarters chose to send an advisor to help us through the investigation and figure out a way to lift the suspensions. The day he arrived, an executive board meeting was held in Mark's room in order to prepare a plan of action. As the New Member Education Chair, I was also requested to attend.

During the meeting my suspicions were confirmed. Apparently, the esteemed Mr. Pwetty Pwease had attempted to do the rock task without the wagon, carrying a large boulder that must have weighed about thirty or forty pounds in his backpack. His resident assistant spotted him struggling with each step as he walked toward his room, and out of responsibility and concern, he asked what was going on. Our pledge readily responded with "it's a task for my fraternity."

"That was a clear form of hazing," the advisor spat out, referring to the rock task.

Afraid of any legal action being thrust toward me personally, I asserted that almost every fraternity at George Mason had a painted rock somewhere on campus, and that we never told him to carry a giant stone in his backpack. That was the very purpose of the Swagger Wagon. I went on to inform him that I had toned down the pledge process quite a bit since I had been named New Member Education Chair and Scholarship Chair of the fraternity, eliminating anything I felt was superfluous or dangerous such as the Beer Mile Run. I also instituted mandatory study halls to ensure they would maintain satisfactory grades and avoid the tragedy that befell my pledge class. But the advisor shocked us all when he revealed that my changes weren't enough.

"You can't have a pledge perform any task that isn't related to learning and being tested on fraternity knowledge." he imparted.

This meant scavenger hunts around campus or D.C. were prohibited, the code activated pledge dances were illicit, and even our pledge uniforms were unlawful. We were all taken aback. We had all expected the advisor to tell us we had done a great job at eliminating the hazing that once took place, but all he did was show us that we didn't know what hazing was. "Technically, even the tests may be against the rules" he muttered as we sat before him, silent in disbelief.

He went on to inform us about the current rules and regulations to run a proper pledge process, but I had already tuned him out. I was both livid and terrified as I was pelted by the barrage of questions that popped into my head one after the other. *How could that damned pledge be so idiotic? Why did I ever become The New Member Educator? Will this come back to bite me?*

Somehow, through the typhoon of uncertainty, I heard the advisor state that we would have initiate the two pledges if they still wanted to join. This caused my anger to bubble up to the point where I couldn't hold it in any longer.

"They aren't fraternity material to begin with. If we had any other options, they would have never even received a bid to join." I declared. Everyone in the room looked toward the ground, embarrassed and in silent agreement.

The advisor from Nationals simply stated "Be that as it may, they became your pledges and now we have to handle the situation as best we can in order to keep this chapter alive. As it sits right now, Nationals is considering the repeal of your charter."

I sat back in my chair, refusing to believe I may be forced to call one of those boobs my brother. *This is ridiculous.* I thought; I could feel myself shut down. This wasn't the AKΛ I decided to join alongside Xavier. This fraternity was more trouble than it was worth; not just shooting itself in the foot at every opportunity, but emptying the clip.

By the meeting's end, I was exhausted and despondent. I walked back to my dorm dragging my feet and staring at the cold cement the entire way. All I could think about was how I should have known AKΛ was a lost cause when they offered me a bid to pledge after I showed no interest in the fraternity life whatsoever. They were desperate long before I even joined. "**You're doomed,**" the voice in my head declared with a chuckle. "**Such a fool,**" it added as it cackled louder.

Once back at my dorm, I went straight to my room, avoiding even Xavier. Trey was sitting at his desk appearing to study, but I was too distraught to pay him any mind as I veered around my desk to reach my bed. He seemed to notice my distress and asked If I was doing okay. I paused as my hands reached the bed; a quick grin graced my face and I chuckled slightly to myself.

Another one huh? I mused before turning back to face him. "I'm just frustrated with working for such a hopeless and unorganized fraternity." I admitted to him while shaking my head and feeling defeated. "We just had a meeting, and I think we just had the final nail placed in our coffin."

Leaning against my bed, I explained to him the troubles I had been having with the group since before I had even been initiated, sharing everything up to even the worries I had about being in legal trouble for any hazing that occurred while I was the New Member Educator. "I didn't even know things like scavenger hunts and making pledges paint a rock were considered hazing!" I reiterated. "I just don't want to end up a scapegoat for AKΛ thanks to my position."

There's no telling how long my rant lasted, but Trey listened the entire time intently. When I was finished he assured me that everything would be fine because I did my best to eliminate what I thought was hazing, and that had to count for something. I was too caught up in a sea of negative thoughts to receive any comfort from this idea, but it was what he suggested next that brought some calm to my spirit.

He said something to the tune of "Just pray on it and I'll pray for you too."

"Thanks." I stammered out, surprised by the suggestion. With the conversation over, I crawled into my bed thinking Trey really was a good guy. I barely even knew him, yet he was going to pray for me. Before that day, I never would have done the same for him, let alone say it. It simply wouldn't have crossed my mind.

As the days went on and we spoke more, I noticed how put together and stable Trey seemed and the positive energy he exuded. He already had an internship at a large insurance firm, his relationship seemed healthy, and every organization he participated in projected him deeper into professional success or spiritual advancement. I wanted that for myself. I needed to know how to obtain the same confidence and self-assurance he emitted every moment I was in his presence.

So, occasionally I would pick his brain and attempt to sneak a peek at what made him so special. In the end I found nothing. In fact, the only difference I found between Trey and I, beyond our age, was that he actively pursued the best avenues available in order to improve himself, while I relegated myself to the paths that opened quickly and with little resistance. Thinking about it, I realized my current job at the mall was the first one to call me in for an interview, and I was accepted into the fraternity based on their own desperation. It even dawned on me that I was granted my positions in the fraternity because no one ran against me, not because I was the best man for the job.

With that in mind, I decided it was time for a change. Folding clothes for pennies wasn't going to get me anywhere, so I applied to every single job I could find related to the field of biology, no matter how minute the connection; everything from research assistant jobs to optometric technician positions. I also began to spend more time on my schoolwork thanks to the cancellation of my weekly pledge classes and my foregoing of the weekly brotherhood meetings.

Coming back from studying to see Nick in our dorm struggling desperately to keep his precious brotherhood alive was quite the depressing sight, but I couldn't bring myself to get involved any further in the organization's troubles. I felt like if I did, I'd be holding myself back. Putting more work into that sinking ship seemed like a fool's gambit at this point. While I would always treasure my friendships and bonds made possible through AKΛ, I was exhausted by the constant shortcomings and failures that erupted at every turn. Most of the brothers of AKΛ were impressive individuals and truly trustworthy men, but as a group there was nothing amazing about them and simple tasks were made onerous. *I've done my best,* I convinced myself, *they'll have to sink or swim on their own.*

Chapter 15

The Witching Hour

Parked beside a chain-link fence that stood adjacent to the road, I was low on gas and holding a predictably dead phone in my hands. It was deep into the night, a little before midnight, in fact, and the roads were eerily silent. Shutting off the headlights of my car left me surrounded by darkness; my only relief being the stars that kindly lent me their glow. I was lost. I took a glimpse around, hoping to find some source of aid, but there wasn't a single person in sight. Asking for directions wasn't an option.

The phone charger in my car was the worst that money could buy. Whether it was a short trip to the grocery store or hours in traffic, no length of time allowed my phone to gain more than two percent of battery life. Even during the long trips up from South Carolina to Fairfax, Virginia it only accomplished the bare minimum: sustaining the current battery level of my phone. Even knowing I needed to buy a new one, I still repeatedly procrastinated. As long as it kept my phone from dying, I didn't feel that it was a very pressing issue.

But now it felt like God was punishing me for my lackadaisical attitude by allowing my phone to perish in the middle of my journey, despite it being connected to a power source for the entire duration. I was stranded in God Knows Where, Northern Virginia, without any means to contact help and no idea how to return to George Mason. For a millisecond, I considered tracing my steps back to Eunice's place to try and get help from Charles, but after so many wrong turns, I couldn't even remember the first one I should make when leaving the dark parking lot that had become my momentary refuge.

Without any options, I leaned my seat back, praying that my charger would be able to give my phone enough juice for me to get some directions back to Mason if I left it alone. I stared at the grey carpeted ceiling of my Camry as I fought to keep my eyelids peeled and vigilant as I waited.

I should have asked Eunice for a charger while I was there. I thought, thinking back to the Thanksgiving dinner that Charles and I had enjoyed at Eunice's house earlier that night. We had gone there directly after spending all of Thanksgiving Day with Charles' family, so I had never found an opportunity to plug in my phone before we arrived. Once in the stranger-filled, unfamiliar environment that was Eunice's home, asking for a charger became an impossible task. I would only speak either when spoken to or when the perfect moment presented itself during conversation, though even then it was highly likely someone more adept at colloquy would speak over me without realizing I had even opened my mouth.

My only course of action was to leave as soon as I had finished my food, and I planned to do just that. With tomorrow being my first big day at my new job, I had the perfect excuse to sneak away early. But of course, before I could dash out the door after throwing away my paper plate, a knock was heard at my would-be exit. It was Eunice's boyfriend, Ryan, coming to wish everyone a happy holiday; his muscular frame filled the width of the doorway, and he had a goofy swagger that was on perfect display as he bounced into the house. *I hate you.* I thought with a twitch in my eye and my mouth agape yet twisted into a grin. *Why is he so damn handsome?*

I watched on as it seemed like the whole family huddled around him. He quickly became the center of attention and the life of the party; a fountain of laughter and joy that no one could resist taking a sip from, not even myself. After Ryan had grabbed a plate and the room had calmed down, Eunice led Ryan, Charles, and me down to the basement. There we sat on the floor and relaxed as Ryan relayed joke after joke and told stories that caused even myself to laugh against my will. I loathed every chuckle that escaped my clamped lips. But I had to admit, though only to myself, he was the better man. *Still hate you.* I mentally reasserted; jealous of this total-package-hunk.

Prying my eyes away from the object of my envy, I looked at my phone to see I only had seven percent battery left. It would be silly to just sit there and let it die, knowing I couldn't get home without it, so I glanced back up to ask my host for a charger. Then, a tap on my shoulder broke my train of thought, and I turned around to see Eunice's sister bent over with a phone charger resting in her palm. I could feel myself blush as I realized how beautiful she looked with her long, jet-black hair draping over her slim face. Her eyes peeked through strands of her hair, such a gentle and enchanting gaze. Her lilac dress caused her already radiant, pecan brown skin to shine that much brighter.

I swallowed nervously and reached for the cord, feeling saved. Suddenly, a lightning bolt of caution struck me; my hand was left hovering over hers. *How did she know I needed a charger? She never saw my phone.*

Furthermore, that lilac dress. Eunice's sister wasn't even wearing one. And come to think of it, she looked nothing like the woman standing in front of me. Hesitantly, I lifted my gaze back up, only to see a gleeful and jagged smile full of knife-like teeth as I felt myself sink into the ground.

***

I gasped for air as my eyes flew open only to see the grey carpeted ceiling of my Camry. "I guess that's what I get for dozing off in the middle of nowhere." I mumbled to myself as I rubbed my eyes, grimacing at the change to my recurring nightmare. No longer were these night terrors confined to a school setting. "I guess all my dreams are free-game now," I grumbled.

Creeped out by having such a dream under a veil of darkness, I looked to my phone for salvation. My face dropped as I saw a measly two percent on the screen, and out of the corner of my eye I could see that forty-five minutes had passed since I had fallen asleep. At that rate, I would have been stuck in that spot until deep in the morning before having enough charge to make it back to campus. For a moment I considered doing just that, staying put and letting my phone's battery dictate when I may leave, but the fact that my gas light had turned on sometime during my nap left my hands tied.

Well, nothing beats a failure but a try. I mused as I threw my car into drive. I pulled out of the parking lot and made my way to the light at the intersection. I prayed as the light turned green, hoping I would make the right choice. Closing my eyes, I slowly pulled forward and attempted to feel the right turn through the ether, quickly opening them as I realized how that was an atrocious idea. My eyes now darted from side to side as I inched through the intersection; right, left, right, left, right and finally back to left. With the traffic lights now behind my car, I was situated directly in the middle of the intersection. I had no choice but to take the left. With my eyes wide open and puffing my cheeks while blowing out a steady stream of air, I hoped I hadn't just wasted my only opportunity to get back before my gas ran out.

Not too far down the road, I found a sign for the highway and decided to take the north ramp. To be honest, I didn't know I had to go North; I didn't even know where I was. I only chose north because Fairfax was located in Northern Virginia. But I guessed correctly, and it wasn't much longer before I had found the exit for Fairfax, which led me to further signs pointing to George Mason.

Thanks to God, luck, and the skin of my teeth, I made it both to a gas station and home. I stared at the clock on my dashboard as I pulled into my parking spot in the lot located behind my building. It was around 1:30 in the morning, so I had less than five hours until I would be back in my car and heading to work. A deep sigh escaped me as I undid my seatbelt and stepped out of my car. I should have been grateful that I made it home safely, but as I ventured through the shadowy abyss cast by the stretch of trees that separated the parking lot from Potomac Heights, I was downtrodden.

Even though I had finally abandoned my job at the mall, the only job I was able to find as a replacement was a seasonal position at the same Target that Brian worked at, and I was certain that was only thanks to his recommendation. I felt like a failure for being unable to find a position on my own, and the job I did secure wasn't related to biology in the slightest. But hell, what did I expect? I couldn't even be responsible enough to keep my phone charged if my life depended on it; an entry level, low-risk retail job was all I deserved.

But enough bellyaching. I resolved; it was time to get myself to bed. I'd need the sleep in order to survive my first Black Friday at a monster retailer. I just prayed that the monster of my dreams had already had its fill of fun earlier, and that I wouldn't be receiving a second visit once my head hit the pillow.

Chapter 16

Patience

After the Christmas season had come and gone, I had been silently let go by Target; the process of which was confusing and emotionally taxing. I knew my position was only seasonal, but during the orientation I was told that some of the best of us were going to be kept on board permanently. I left for Christmas break assuming that, by some miracle, I was selected as one of the lucky few since there was no indication that I had been let go, but after finding out I hadn't been scheduled for any shifts after January first, I became worried. I asked Brian if he had heard anything, but he was clueless. I called my Target location to see what was going on, and they seemed just as oblivious; not just about my employment status, but about who I even was. It was like I had been erased not only from the schedule, but from the company's history. In my mind, the interactions with my former managers confirmed my worst fear: I left so little of an impression that they had forgotten I existed the moment I left the building for vacation.

I already knew I was a disappointing hire from the jump. I wasn't a liability, but I was so unsure of what I should be doing or how to prioritize on the job, that I could often be found wandering nervously back and forth between the sales floor and the back room, searching for just the tiniest morsel of direction. Furthermore, I was completely incapable of speaking to any of my peers on the job, save Brian, without my voice quavering or avoiding eye contact. I knew quite well this diffidence would be my downfall, so when I was told about my fate by a representative from Human Resources, I was disappointed, but far from surprised.

Unfortunately, the news came too late, and my bus ticket back to GMU had already been purchased. So even though I was jobless and there were still weeks left until the spring semester would begin, I found myself back in a nearly vacant Potomac Heights on January fifth. With my ever-dwindling reserve of cash starting to become a concern, I took advantage of the ample free time and searched for new positions online. But each job description served only to discourage me, making me realize that my personality was not cut out for the retail or serving jobs that I was qualified for. Out of frustration, I'd occasionally rest my head on the edge of the desk, only to see the pile of used hookah vapes that rested mockingly in the waste basket below. It was as if they were chastising me for spending the lion's share of my income on such a useless, though redolent, vice.

The solitude and quiet of our dorm became an echo chamber for my troubles, threatening to drive me insane unless I found a solution. The dorm felt especially empty since Trey had moved out after graduating in December, and his side of the room now sat naked and barren. Both Nick and Xavier had also left for the holidays, lending to the initial stagnant and noiseless environment, but once Xavier learned I wasn't going to be working for the rest of the winter break as planned, he came back to campus early for some much needed "bro-time." This period was when one of our favorite pastimes was born: Drunk Zombies.

These were boozy nights at home where we'd be found playing Zombie mode on Call of Duty until our skill diminished and our gameplay was reduced to randomly mashing buttons. Once we were too intoxicated to start up a new round, we tossed the game aside in order to partake in a session of our ever-alluring Special Hookah, during which we would spew fuddled complaints about relationships, college, and any other inconvenience that life had decided to throw at us that day. Eventually we'd retire back upstairs to our dorm, and I'd head straight to my room, throw myself onto my reformed Mega-Bed, and choose a random flavor from my pile of disposable hookahs I continued to buy in bulk online despite my waning funds. The remainder of my night would be spent staring blankly at the haze released from my lungs as it rose to the plain white ceiling and carried me to dreamland.

But even my vices and these cathartic sessions of Drunken Zombies with Xavier couldn't quell the uneasiness I felt. It was like standing at the edge of a sinking cruise ship and watching the water engulf my rapidly disappearing sanctuary, pulling me closer to the deadly and freezing ocean below. I couldn't drink away the fact that in just one year I'd be preparing to graduate, and I wasn't even capable of holding down a simple retail job.

Luckily, a detoxifying break from our bender was coming up. It was the thirteenth of January, four days after my twenty-first birthday, and we were heading to New York City. Xavier had planned to visit his father during our winter vacation, and, not wanting to make the four-hour bus trip from Union Station in D.C. to the Big Apple alone, he invited me to come along. Since I didn't have a job to attend to, I had no reason not to oblige. Furthermore, I thought getting off that campus was exactly what we needed. I'd get time away from my looming reality, and Xavier would get a well-earned break away from the hardships of his long-burning, dumpster-fire relationship with Amanda. It was a win-win situation.

At least that was what we believed in the beginning. It turns out that during a four-hour bus ride in a cabin that reeks of piss and cigarette smoke, you can run out of lively topics of conversation rather quickly. Muted stillness filled the bus once the greyhound reached the highway and the journey had truly gotten underway. Only the indiscernible whispers and hushed coughs of other passengers could be heard throughout the cabin. By the second hour, my phone had died, unsurprisingly, and Xavier and I naturally broke the silence with the usual discussion of our woes; though now in a painfully sober context.

Xavier opened up first, asking me what I thought about his relationship with Amanda. Their first anniversary had recently passed in December, and things weren't developing as he had always dreamed. It wasn't that the relationship had simply lost its luster, or the magic had disappeared. It wasn't just that the rose-colored glasses had been flung off by time. It was something far worse; he confided that the relationship felt like a farce. "I know relationships take work and patience," he mused "but this feels like we are on life support. Like we are together just for the sake of being together. I don't even believe she is really attracted to me."

I stared back at him with my eyebrows raised and my eyes wide. A single elongated and sharp whistle escaped my lips as I stalled for time. I wasn't sure how honest I should be. *What would I want to hear from him if I were in his situation?* I pondered. I looked away and surveyed the bus, slightly embarrassed by the serious turn our conversation was going to take while in earshot of other travelers. I looked back to Xavier, and he was peering at me, still awaiting my response. I took in a deep, meditative breath and said, "I think you are wasting each other's time," having settled on complete honesty.

Xavier and Amanda shared fundamental differences that I couldn't foresee them ever overcoming. Amanda never wanted to get married, Xavier looked forward to that very permanent and beautiful union. Amanda never wanted to own a house, preferring the freedom renting provided, while Xavier simply desired a permanent home. When I met Xavier, he had wanted children, but Amanda made it very clear she never wished to be pregnant. Neither of them shared any hobbies beyond the very basics: TV, movies, drinking, and music. Now he was telling me she didn't seem attracted to him. That the kisses they shared felt more like polite and obligatory greetings than something that sprung up out of love and affection. I couldn't bring myself to lie to him.

"I only see this ending in heartbreak for you." I told him as I looked up hesitantly. "If I were you, I'd rip that band-aid off now." He turned away from me and looked out the large bus window, his meditative pout clear in the reflection. It seemed my statement had struck a chord.

After a few moments, he turned back and asked "but what if things can get better? People can change. It might just be a matter of patience."

"Maybe." I admitted while peering down at the floor of the bus. "But you both couldn't make it three months without running into irreconcilable issues. And now you're not sure if she is even attracted to you? I don't think any amount of waiting can fix that."

We both sat in silence for a minute or so after that. Obviously, the conversation had reached a point where further discussion could only serve to put a dark cloud over our short vacation to New York.

Looking to change the subject, Xavier asked me how my job search had been going. "Same as usual" I shot out with a sigh. "I don't care what it is, I just want something even marginally related to science so I can get some experience, but at this point it seems hopeless."

"What do you want to do after you graduate?" he questioned. "I hear you talk about working in science or in a hospital all the time, but is there anything you want to do, specifically? Anything you're passionate about?"

"Nope." The answer had escaped my lips before I could even think about it. "Any respectable job that pays enough is fine with me. I just happen to enjoy biology."

"Really? Nothing in particular piques your interest at all?" Xavier probed.

With an awkward smile and nervously scratching the top of my head I muttered "Not really. Sometimes I wish I was more like you, knowing that you want to help people. The only thing I've ever cared about is finding someone I could love and shower with all my affection; someone that would do the same for me in turn. A partner for life that I could start a family with." The mere thought made me feel warm and fluffy inside.

Xavier smiled and said, "That does sound nice man."

"Yeah man." I responded. "Besides my family and friends, it's the only thing that has ever mattered to me. Kind of a pathetic life goal, right?" I tried my best to laugh off the discomfort that crept up every time I thought about the fact that I had no other passions. It was all I could do to prevent myself from spiraling into a crisis. I could feel panic surging through my body as a single question echoed from my very soul:

"Why do you even exist?"

My face must have betrayed my inner conflict, as Xavier responded by leaning in his seat, turning his gaze to his lap, and stating "We're not too different. I don't really know what I want to do either. Helping people is super broad and I only chose to major in therapeutic recreation based on some career assessment I took freshman year." He paused for a moment and looked at me with a goofy grin as he added "We'll figure everything out with time. And if not, we'll just have to bumble our way through life together."

A weak smile crossed my face as a feeling of appreciation replaced the anxiety that filled my being only moments ago. Sadly, that sweet feeling itself was abruptly replaced by a feeling of disgust and nausea as a strong whiff of urine entered my nostrils as if someone had freshly relieved themselves. "I hate buses." I declared, causing Xavier to chuckle as he watched me shrink my face into my hoodie to avoid the offensive scent. *Please let us reach Port Authority soon.* I prayed as I closed my eyes and attempted to ignore my surroundings.

***

Later that night, once we had settled into a cozy room on the second floor of Xavier's father's home in Queens, I sat on the edge of one of the short twin beds that filled up most of the minikin space. I was tired from the restless trip, but I wanted to check the notifications I had missed while on the bus. As my screen lit up, I saw a missed call symbol strewn across the top. Clicking on it, I became puzzled by the unfamiliar phone number, but I decided to listen to the voicemail anyway. It was Visionworks, one of the eyeglass retailers I had applied to. They wanted to know if I was still interested in the optometric technician position, and when I could come in for an interview. I closed my eyes in relief; things were finally looking up.

Chapter 17

Down in The Gully

The summer of 2014, I learned the true meaning of heartbreak, the bona fide definition of pain, and the wretchedness that is dejection. There I was in my car, eyes wide open and my mouth agape; unable to turn my gaze away from the scene unfolding before me. I felt as if I had been holding onto the love of my life over a fathomless ravine as she slipped out of my weakening grip. The sharp rocks below voraciously waited to claim her life and the river gleefully prepared to carry the remains out of sight. My lover tells me it's okay to let go and pulls herself from my grip and falls; resigned to her fate.

I reached out futilely to prevent the tragedy from reaching its certain end, but as my cookie finally hit the muddy floor of my car, it was like watching that imaginary lover hit those menacing boulders at the foot of the cliff. Like thunder punctuating the misfortune that had just occurred, my stomach gnarled.

That cookie would have been the dessert to my only meal of the day: a $5 fill up box from KFC that consisted of a Famous Bowl, a drink, and the aforementioned cookie that was lost before her time. Despite the hefty bowl of mashed potatoes, corn, and popcorn chicken, I still needed a little something more to top myself off. I stared at that chocolate chip cookie as it laid on the dirty floor, debating whether to give into my carnal desires and throw the cookie down my gullet. I picked up the cookie and stared at it wistfully before tossing it out the window to remove the temptation. "Damn it." I hissed as I turned the key and started my car in order to escape the KFC parking lot that had been the scene of my recent catastrophe. "May as well mope at home."

This summer, my humble abode was the new home that a few brothers from our chapter had started renting at the end of the spring semester. At some point during the second half of the school year, the dust had settled and the suspensions on our fraternity had been lifted thanks to the efforts of Nick as our new President, and other key members such as Garrett and Brian. I myself had tuned out from the fraternity at this point and was, for all intents and purposes, simply a butt filling a chair that had no idea what efforts went into the feat of keeping our withering group alive. In contrast, Nick still believed in the fraternity fervently, and his first order of business was to reinvent AKΛ's worsening image at George Mason. What better way to accomplish this, than getting our Beta Chi chapter its own unofficial house? A central and dedicated location for parties, rush events, meetings, and more.

The house suited our ever-shrinking club perfectly in both body and spirit. Though the house sat at the crossroads of two main streets, Braddock Road and Union Mill Road, it felt almost cut off from the rest of the world. The house was imperceptible from the street due to out-of-control vegetation and the entrance to it's all but hidden driveway being situated awkwardly in the middle of a right turn lane.

After successfully making the sudden turn into the driveway hidden in the shadows created by overgrown plant life, one would find themselves in front of a worn, double- leaf wire gate held closed by a simple latch. From the front of the gate, one could see nothing but more towering grass, weeds, and what appeared to be cattails mixed in. There were no signs of human life except the asphalt of the driveway leading you through the threshold and down a steep hill. To anyone unfamiliar with the house, it was a scene that screamed drug den or murderer's hideout, but the driveway was so thin that turning around wasn't an option. The only choices were to reverse dangerously into the turn lane behind, or continue following the path into the darkness, praying you could turn around and floor it back to the main road before coming in contact with the dangers within.

But those brave enough to venture through the gate and down the ominous hill surrounded by wild flora and tall trees would be greeted by a quaint little two-story white cottage. Emphasis on the word "little", as the ceilings inside were so low that guests over six feet tall were forced to bend their necks in order to avoid dragging and bumping their heads against them as they walked around the house. It reminded me of how I'd always pictured the old home belonging to the grandmother of Little Red Riding Hood. That is, if she had beer cans discarded carelessly on her front porch, and a large driveway that was more akin to a parking lot. Among members of our fraternity, this house was known by many names; The White House and The Alamo being fan favorites. But I preferred a different, and in my opinion more accurate, name: The Gully.

On the day of my gastronomic mishap, I was reminded why I felt that epithet fit so well. As I returned from my disappointing meal, my stomach still writhing from hunger, I parked my car in that overly large driveway and grimaced upon stepping into a deep puddle of water that remained after the showers from the night before. You see, thanks to the steep hills surrounding the entirety of the property, any rain that chose to fall on it rushed down the slopes, practically flooding the land around The Gully. Large pools of water formed in the driveway with the slightest drizzle, and the usually dry spots of dead grass on the unkempt lawn became muddy pits.

Rolling my eyes at myself for the rookie mistake, I carefully stepped over the puddle with my remaining dry foot and began to rush inside to change my sock. As I approached the main front door, I looked over to another entrance on my right which led to the in-law suite where Brian stayed, wondering if he was home since the house was uncharacteristically quiet for an evening in a frat house. Even if it was the summer, it was rare to have a quiet moment in the home. I was too concerned with my empty belly and my wet sock to ponder the question for long though, and made my way into the house.

Instantly my hunger pains disappeared as I opened the door and was hit with the smell of feces and urine that permeated the air, reminding me of our guests and the disarray hidden within The Gully's cozy, cottage-in-the-woods facade. The dishes piled up in the kitchen sink, riddled with rotting food, the garbage strewn throughout the home as if the house itself was a trash bin, and the insects of all types feasting on the buffet were only the tip of the revolting iceberg. The state of the place always made my skin crawl and prevented me from even considering the idea of eating within those walls, let alone cooking.

But surprisingly, the nauseating chaos of the house was not the source of the smell that tormented my nostrils daily. No, the source of this pungent odor was the pet rat of a girl staying in Caleb's room while he was back home in Arizona for the summer. From the intensity of the smell, I could only assume the cage had never been cleaned, and every drop and drip the pest excreted must have sat collecting at the bottom. Due to the lack of air conditioning in all parts of the house except for my room and the heat of the season, the smell was made all the more powerful and persistent as the days passed, to the point where even the air began to develop a slight but notable vile flavor.

For that very reason I tended to lock myself in my room with the AC set to the highest possible setting, an air freshener plugin always sitting in the outlet, and a towel pressed against the lower door gap; everything I could do to keep the sour, fecal odor at bay. And that day was no different. While breathing as little as possible, I rushed up the dingy and creaky, tan-carpeted steps to the second floor, turned to the left, and flew through the first doorway which led to my room, slamming the door behind me. After the towel had been fully squeezed into its place at the bottom of the door and I was certain the air was saturated with the fragrance of apple cinnamon once again, I allowed myself to breathe normally and laid down on the queen-sized air mattress that sat in the center of the mostly barren room; the only other occupants being two suitcases that contained all my belongings and a laptop laying on the floor. That bed brought me all the comfort I needed to push through to the next day each and every night. It was the shining light in my painfully uncomfortable summer that began the moment I realized keeping my position at Visionworks meant forgoing the typical, long summer vacation at my parents' home.

I had convinced myself the work experience would be worth it, despite having nowhere to stay during the sweltering summer months. I thought sleeping in my car wouldn't be too bad, since I could always get a gym membership and use the showers in the locker room. Initially, I didn't consider The Gully as a viable option because all of the rooms were spoken for, but as luck would have it, Nick would save me from my vagrant scheme. He was going back home to Virginia Beach for the summer, and he wasn't too keen on paying rent on a room he wasn't occupying. He offered me his room for the entirety of the break, and I accepted without hesitation, successfully gaining a roof over my head.

Unfortunately, all I had to sleep on when I moved in was a sleeping bag loaned to me by Xavier, and my twin sized bed set I used in the dorms. With no other recourse, I slept on the floor like a squatter.

Even worse, most of the money I earned at my part-time position with Visionworks went towards the rent, for the room I quickly learned I truly couldn't afford. The rest was quickly consumed by other household bills, leaving me with very little to spend on anything beyond gas to go to work, and one meal a day.

But then, upon hearing about my living conditions, a hero rose, lifting my spirits during that impoverished and laborious interlude between semesters. This was the person that had lent me the air mattress; that had pulled me out of the sleeping bag and off the floor. This liberator was the true reason a mere bed filled with air brought me so much comfort and peace. This savior was my girlfriend, Madison.

As I laid on my loaner air mattress, battling the sandman while staring at my phone, I thought back to our very first date, and how much I couldn't wait to be with her again. It had been a few weeks since I had seen her last, so I decided to send her a text, asking if she could make some time for me. But before she could respond, the sandman won our bout.

***

Suddenly, I came to my senses in the middle of a familiar scene within a restaurant. Madison was on my left and Xavier and Amanda sat opposite us. We were sitting in a booth at the end of what appeared to be a more than gratifying meal at the Cheesecake Factory, if the signage and empty plates were any clue. Looking out the window, I could see the inner harbor of Baltimore, Maryland. I was puzzled as to how I got there until I heard Xavier guffaw boisterously while raising his glass. "Who said nothing good comes from being sad and drunk!" Xavier jested as everyone laughed and he began to recount how our double date had come to be. I giggled to myself, realizing what was happening. I was dreaming about my first date with Madison.

When I wasn't suffering from my recurring nightmare, many of my dreams were like this: crystal clear and life-like. Whether I was dreaming about an epic battle in a post-apocalyptic world against gangs that threatened my family, or simply dreaming that I had mysteriously gained the ability to float two feet in the air, my dreams were lucid, granting me control of everything around me. In my dream against the gangs, I felt the epic battle deserved rolling credits, and so it was. In my dream where I could float only feet above the ground, I whimsically skirted around campus while taunting men who were still glued to the ground, and seducing women with ease. So, in this dream about my first date with my curly-headed lover, I simply let it play out to the end.

Xavier sang the tale of how I had met Madison on Tinder after I had downloaded the app during a particularly wild night of Drunk Zombies in February. A night that left me feeling desperate enough to give online dating a try. I knew what Tinder was meant for at the time, but I was a hopeless romantic taking a shot in the dark for love. By some stroke of luck, I hit my target. It was a petite white girl, with thick and curly, dirty blonde hair. She was sporty with a laid-back personality and a boisterous laugh that was accompanied by the occasional snort; it felt like receiving a gold star in kindergarten every time I could pull it out of her with a solid joke.

Due to having the confidence of a prairie dog, and despite the memory of my date with Eunice one year ago, I once again turned to Xavier and Amanda to come along and make our first outing a double date. Xavier expressed that he was relieved this date went according to plan, and that Amanda and Madison got along so strikingly well; to the point where they were making clever quips at our expense. In contrast to the year before, the air was full of excitement, love, and witty banter.

Once Xavier finished retelling the story, the dream skipped ahead to the end of the double date. We had decided to take a stroll around the harbor and enjoy the cool, early-spring air before heading back to our cars. Xavier and Amanda seemed more in love than ever before. Amanda held his hand tightly and clutched her body against his, as if mimicking the body language of Madison and I. The gleam in everyone's eyes and the goofy grins announced the night's success to every passerby.

After we said our goodbyes to Amanda and Xavier, the dream skipped ahead even further. Now we were sitting on the couch in Madison's apartment, watching something random on the television. My arm was wrapped around her shoulders as her head rested gently on my chest. I looked at my watch, and realized it was probably best that I left; I didn't want to overstay my welcome. At that moment, my heart began to beat a thousand times a second as I planned my exit, and a million times faster than that after I realized she could probably hear, if not feel, every single time my anxious heart pounded against my chest. I wanted to kiss her before leaving. *But how? Her head is on my chest. I can't lean in from this position.* I thought. *How could I...*

In that instant she turned her head towards me and kissed me gently without saying a single word. The kiss lasted only a second, but to a young man that hadn't felt the touch of a woman in over a year, it was like being transported to a dimension where time and space held no power, and only ecstasy existed. She pulled back and told me I didn't have to drive home that night; it was getting too late.

Without a second thought I agreed and followed her down the hall, toward her room, while I smiled like an idiot behind me as if there was a camera crew recording the entire date. After I passed the threshold, the door closed, and the dream faded to black while giggles could be heard from behind the white entryway.

***

I woke up beaming like an idiot at that reminder of a simple night that ended with more kisses than I could count. It was such a perfect date, that the only improvement the director of my dreams could make to the scenes of my memory was the omission of hours spent driving in the maddening traffic of the Baltimore area.

Rubbing some sand out of my eye, I grabbed my phone that had fallen to the side to see if I had missed a reply from my beloved. As I turned on the screen, I realized it had been a couple hours since I fell asleep. Panic rose from within me as I realized I may have missed my opportunity. She was a busy college girl with a lot of friends and a part-time job working at a bison farm, so sometimes it was hard for her to make time for me. That was the reason I drove to her most of the time, and why she had only driven down to see me on two or three occasions since the day I had met her. It was hard enough for her to lock down time for a Skype date or phone call, so asking her to add a one-and-a-half-hour drive to her day was too much.

After scanning my screen, it became clear that there was nothing to worry about, as there wasn't a single message on my phone. Crestfallen, I sent her a message telling her I was going to bed, I hoped she had a good day, and that I loved her. I set my phone face down and to the side in order to avoid the temptation of checking it every five minutes. I hoped my patience would be rewarded, and that I'd wake up to a loving message from my girlfriend.

To my chagrin, I wouldn't receive a single reply from her until halfway through the next day while I was sitting in the backroom at Visionworks. It read: "Maybe, I haven't decided what I'm going to do this weekend yet."

"Of course, she can't commit again." I murmured to myself while gritting my teeth. "Why do I let myself get excited?"

I reread Madison's message again and again. "That's all you have to say to me after not seeing each other for weeks? At least sound like you miss me!" I groaned to myself;

the pink of my nails turning white as I clasped my phone like a vise.

But clinging to the memory of that first date and burying my frustrations under the hope that things would get easier in the future, I took a calming breath and got back to work with a forced, retail-worker smile on my face. I was finally on the road to getting everything I had ever wished for in life; how could I give up on it? Even if it felt like there was an imp on my shoulder, cracking up and yelling "**she doesn't love you!**" repeatedly into my ear, I had to stay the course.

Chapter 18

Head in the Clouds

Pulling in the sweet smoke of Special Hookah and allowing the gummy bear vapors to fill my lungs was the simplest joy I had felt in a long time. Slowly releasing the haze as it rose to the stars and appreciating the shimmer and dance of the sparks on the red-hot coals during a cold, clear January night felt like the purest ecstasy. Before the cloud of smoke dissipated, I was already back at the hose for more, watching the bubbles form in the reservoir with the same delight as a child blowing air into his soda through his straw.

"Can't believe you gave this up for Madison, huh?" Xavier jived as he saw my face of elation and peace.

I nodded my head in agreement while allowing the second drag of smoke to saturate my lungs. As I passed the hose to Charles, I responded through clouds of smoke exiting my mouth, "I should have followed my instincts when she told me she would break up with me on the spot if she ever found out I had *smoked* before."

"Desperation will have you doing crazy things and ignoring red flags," Charles chimed. "You really wanted to make it work."

"You don't know the half of it man," I joked while laughing at myself and stroking my chin; the stubble of my freshly regrown beard felt particularly pleasant against the tips of my fingers as the hookah slowly took effect. "You should have seen all of the things I tried to ignore and fix in our relationship over the past few months."

***

September and October

While sleeping in the basement of Madison's family home, a sharp creak from the stairs startled me awake. My eyes shot open, and I was greeted by a dimly lit figure standing in the darkness; one foot stood on the bottom step, while the other rested on the basement floor. It had one hand delicately resting on the banister, and the other hanging freely. With only the indirect light of bathroom at the bottom of the steps illuminating the figure, I was only able to discern one thing: that it belonged to a woman. I sprang up excitedly, believing Madison had snuck down in the middle of the night for some late-night fun. It was the last thing I would have expected from her since she wasn't one for big romantic gestures, so I wasn't going to waste another second staring at her outline.

But as I began scooching toward the edge of my bed, the figure moved closer into the light, and I noticed it had long dark straight hair. This wasn't Madison at all. I was so shocked I could do nothing but watch. It was as if I was frozen in place with my eyes stapled open. As my mysterious visitor continued walking vixenishly toward the bathroom, the light revealed there was only a pink towel loosely wrapped around her that was preventing me from seeing her unclad body.

I tried to yell out and ask her what she was doing there, but there was nothing but silence. At that moment, finally poised directly under the light of the bathroom with her back facing me, she dropped the towel, baring her olive skin for all to see. This felt wrong. I wanted to shut my eyes and turn away, but I couldn't. As if some carnal force prevented me.

Finally, as she began to turn toward me, I recognized her face. It was Madison's best friend, Taylor. I felt guilt rain down on me like fist-sized hail, and finally mustered the strength to swivel my eyes to my right. There, squatting weightlessly at the edge of the air mattress, was the grey-skinned witch smiling in all of her jagged-fanged glory; her decrepit and feeble looking arm extended towards me and reaching over my head. Suddenly, I could feel her large, bony grey hand holding my cranium in place; her nails dug into my eyelids to keep them peeled. Frozen in place and unable to speak, I could do nothing as her hand began pressing downward. I felt my body start to sink into an icy pool of darkness emanating from the bed. In vain, I attempted to scream "Please, not the cave again!" but not even the slightest squeak escaped my lips. Until the moment the eerie shadows engulfed me entirely, my gaze was fixed on her mischievous and unending grin.

***

Heaving as if I had just outrun the devil himself, I kept my eyes clenched shut while praying I was back in the waking world. My entire body was drenched in the usual cold sweat and my hands were clasping my sheets. Finding the courage to open one eye, I peeked across the room and noticed my roommate Leon was still sleeping soundly. *Thank God I never wake up screaming.* I thought as I started getting up to change my sweat soaked shirt. Then, as soon as I put weight on my right leg, a deep and sharp pain shot up and nearly caused me to collapse. Biting down on my bottom lip, I somehow managed to contain my screech. After my nightmare, I had completely forgotten I had injured my leg in a naive attempt to impress Madison.

Madison loved running, and she had been part of both the track and cross-country teams during her high school days. I thought showing an interest in her hobbies would help to improve our relationship that was currently sailing through rocky waters, so I proposed we do a zombie run together for Halloween. Her response was less than enthused, and her usual excuse raised its ugly head: she wasn't sure if she'd be free since she would be busy all throughout October.

Not one to give up, I searched high and low for another race that would be more convenient for her. This led me to a 5k that was not only scheduled for late September, but, most importantly, would be held less than twenty minutes from her apartment. I hurried to confirm with her that it was on a day that she didn't work, and, with no excuse at hand, she let me sign us both up. Sadly, even though Madison always told me she was excited as the number of weeks before the run declined, she couldn't mask her lack of enthusiasm. She never wanted to help me train, she constantly forgot the date of the race, and any time it was brought up, she'd grumble and warn that "something may come up."

I told myself she was simply being pessimistic due to her packed schedule, and I trained passionately for weeks in preparation, constantly sharing my progress and hoping my eagerness would eventually become contagious. The thought of making Madison smile as she ran at my side helped me to push through the wheezing and the cramping. Of course, Madison didn't hesitate to teach that ardor can't be forced down someone's throat. The day before the race, Madison let me know that she had offered to cover a shift at the bison farm. Coincidentally, the shift would start just a couple of hours after the race would begin, so, since the farm was roughly an hour away from the racetrack, she'd be dropping out of the 5k. She didn't want to risk arriving late by choosing to compete.

The relief in her voice was so poorly veiled I couldn't deny it any longer; she never wanted to run a 5k with me to begin with. Livid but determined not to waste weeks of training, I resigned myself to just running the race on my own. My only request was that she let me stay the night at her place so I could avoid an exhausting drive of nearly two hours the same day as the run. She agreed, and told me I could sleep on the floor.

As I was getting prepared the morning of, out of the blue, Madison announced she had changed her mind. Her new plan was to head straight to work from the finish line and skip the majority of the final ceremony. Maybe it was guilt; maybe she felt her excuse was paper thin. She never expressed the reason she had such a change of heart, but I could tell she felt forced in some way by the way she still carried herself in a lackadaisical manner as if hoping we could miss the registration time if she moved just a bit too slowly.

Regardless, I was so overjoyed I wasn't tackling the race alone that I ran faster than I ever had before, winning second place in my age group. Slowly though, the sense of joy and personal accomplishment from the silver painted medal on my chest was replaced with regret as a pain in my right quadriceps grew more intense once the adrenaline had worn off. I had forgotten to stretch before the race, and I was going to pay the price. The pain grew to the point where putting weight on my right leg was nearly impossible, and I had to limp everywhere I walked. Even weeks later, simply walking over to the wardrobe in the center of the room to change my clothes, it felt as if several knives were being plunged deep into the muscles of my leg with every step.

Once I had changed my clothes and made it back into my bed, my efforts to fall back asleep were thwarted by flashes of the witch grinning inches away from my face. The pain in my leg every time I tossed and turned did nothing to help my situation either. My thoughts bounced between the

5k and the apparition that had haunted my dreams since I was a child. *Why has the dream been changing after all these years? Why did I try so hard in that race to begin with? Why did I dream of her friend Taylor, and not Madison herself?*

I racked my brain for what felt like hours. I hoped the answers would purge the images of the sorceress and her damned cave from my mind, and allow me to sleep peacefully. Eventually, I thought back to a message Madison had sent me not too long ago after I had met her friend Taylor for the first time. She said Taylor had told her "Your boyfriend is sexy."

I half chuckled to myself. I was so desperate for affection in my own relationship, that a single innocent and indirect complement was all it took for a woman I barely knew to enter my fantasies. I hadn't heard those words from Madison in months, and was saddened that the only time in recent memory she had made me feel attractive, was when she was merely quoting her friend. After that, my brain went into a frenzy. Comparing the way we kissed when we met to how forced it felt currently; the way she used to flirt, to the cold way she treated my advances months into our relationship. I bit down on the tip of my thumb once my brain came to the only logical conclusion: Madison isn't attracted to me anymore. *I have to fix this,* I thought. *I have to bring back our spark.*

October and November

"Wait, so you never go home for Thanksgiving?" Madison questioned vehemently, seemingly appalled at the discovery of my college Thanksgiving tradition.

"Yeah, I always go to Charles' house to spend it with his family." I responded, stunned by her animated reply. "I always work and I'm never able to take enough vacation days to make the twenty-four-hour bus ride home worth it."

"You can just take a plane then. There's no excuse." Madison asserted while shaking her head in protest.

"I'm afraid of heights though." I stammered; slightly frightened by the passion in Madison's eyes that was a rare sight as of late. "I've never been on a plane by myself before, and I never will if I can avoid it." I paused for a moment before continuing. I knew what her response to my next sentence would be, well before it had even left my lips, but nothing beats a failure except a try. "Maybe I could do it if you went with me. I'd buy the tickets of course." I squeaked out.

Madison raised an eyebrow as if confused by the proposal; the slight hint of a smile still crossing her face. "I guess I can go with you." she said tenderly, allowing her sweet smile to shine.

In response, my eyebrows raised in astonishment. *Did she just agree to go with me?* I asked myself. I didn't expect her to concede so easily. She was supposed to say "no" in order to free me from both the obligation of sitting in a flying deathtrap and paying for the tickets with jacked up holiday prices.

Still, I was beyond thrilled to know that Madison wanted to come down to meet my family for Thanksgiving. *Did she think we were at a point where she should meet my family?* I mused. I'd never brought a girlfriend home before, so I was already fantasizing about the wondrous moment we got off the plane and my family would rush up to meet my potential wife and shower us with love, welcoming Madison with such warmth that she couldn't help but feel like she belonged.

Sadly, my fantasy was cut short when Madison continued. "But I would need to be back home by Thanksgiving." she clarified.

I furrowed my brow as I searched for the logic in her statement. At best we'd be able to leave for my parents' home on the Tuesday before Thanksgiving. That would mean she would either be spending less than a day with my family and leaving on Wednesday, or she would have to travel early in the morning on Thanksgiving Day to be home in time to celebrate with her own family.

"So, you couldn't spend Thanksgiving with my family" I meekly confirmed. "Even if it meant traveling the day of?"

"Oh no, of course not, I just wanted to make sure you could get home and spend time with your family for the holiday!" she exclaimed, giggling and pushing my shoulder in jest. "And obviously I'd want to be with my own family too."

I laughed with her and accepted the conditions while my heart wretched on the inside. Madison didn't care about meeting my family at all. She was simply passionate about families being together during the holidays and was willing to go the extra mile in order to unite mine like some sort of holiday angel. It was a noble venture, but I couldn't help but feel slighted.

I had already planned to spend Christmas with her family after being invited, choosing to sacrifice time with my family so I could strengthen the bonds with my potential, future in-laws. In contrast, Madison didn't think for a second about spending Thanksgiving Day with my family. It wasn't an option in her book. Even after seven months of dating, it was clear she had never considered the idea that my family could one day become her own.

One month later, on the morning of Thanksgiving Day, I couldn't help but tear up at the distance growing between us, both literally and figuratively, as I watched my girlfriend pass through security at the Columbia Airport. Despite the efforts of my family to show her a fun and relaxing time, the look on Madison's face during her day in the Drayton Home could be described by a single word: Vacant. Sure, she would give a smirk here, and a polite grin there, but there was no soul behind them. At the airport, she wore nothing but a shining smile so huge that it could be seen clearly as she waved goodbye from beyond the security checkpoint, like a lighthouse on a foggy night at sea. It was a smile that had become foreign to me. *What am I doing wrong?* I wondered. *Why can't she smile like that with me, even though she says she loves me?*

December

Around 11:00 at night on New Year's Eve, Madison and I were standing in her family's kitchen while enjoying some wine coolers and mixed drinks while we waited for Xavier and Amanda to arrive. Originally, they were supposed to have arrived three hours prior, but Amanda's disappearance threw a wrench in those plans. Amanda had spent the first part of New Year's Eve with her own friends, and seemingly opted to ignore every message Xavier had sent throughout the day. At first Xavier assumed she hadn't been looking at her phone, but he started to panic once she didn't come home at 6:00pm as planned and prepared to cancel our plans in order to scour all of Mason to find her. Then, suddenly, at the exact moment he placed his hand on the doorknob to begin his search, the door pushed him back. Standing on the other side was Amanda who had finally decided to come home at 8:00pm; the time when they should have been arriving at Madison's house.

"Are your friends still coming? It's almost midnight" Madison inquired. I honestly wasn't sure anymore. Xavier had gone dark after telling me he had found Amanda. Even if they had left at 8:30pm, he should have arrived by 10:30pm at the latest.

I bumbled my phone out of my pocket, still no message from Xavier. With no response from Amanda either, I started to grow worried. Madison's family lived in the boonies of Maryland; *What if some barbaric bigots saw them?* I speculated nervously to myself. There were a couple streets frequented by local racists that Madison's mom had cautioned me to avoid, so my concern for the interracial couple wasn't unjustified.

As I started to bite my nails from the stress, a knock at the door calmed my paranoia instantly. As expected, it was Xavier and Amanda, but something was off. Amanda had a huge smile on her face that sang "all's right with the world", while Xavier's expression was stern, as if he was hiding a storm within. Immediately, Xavier asked me where the drinks were in a monotone voice I had never heard from him before. Feeling the urgency, I swiftly showed him to the kitchen, and we began taking shots and drinking to our hearts content as if we were back in our pledging days.

One minute from midnight, the girls joined the rest of Madison's family in the living room to get ready for the countdown. The moment they were out of earshot, I turned to ask Xavier what had happened during those three mysterious hours of radio silence, but before I could utter a word, and without facing me, he nonchalantly announced: "Amanda and I broke up."

I was stunned and befuddled; I stood in place examining Xavier's expression until everyone in the living room started the New Year's Countdown. I joined in, but I was so dazed by what I was told only moments before, that every number came out as a whisper. Even after the countdown from ten reached its end and 2015 had begun, I was too consumed in my own thoughts to enthusiastically cheer for the New Year.

My perplexed state was not due to the fact that Amanda and Xavier had decided to end the relationship. Rather it was born from the awkwardness of Amanda's presence. After a few moments had passed, I asked the one question in my head that screamed to be released louder than any other. "So why is she here?"

Xavier took in a deep breath, and with jaded eyes he looked into my own before stating, "Not sure. We broke up before we even started the drive here. After everything was said and done she asked me if *we* were still spending New Years with you all. I was so stunned by the audacity I just said yes." Xavier paused as he looked in Amanda's direction. She was chatting and giggling with Madison as if nothing had happened. "The worst part is I don't think she cares one bit. Two years down the drain, and she's laughing over there like a hyena."

Xavier bit down on his bottom lip and clenched his fist as if holding back tears; quietly, he unleashed a barrage of questions that seemed to have plagued him the entire drive there: "Why did she beg me to go to relationship counseling with her? Why did she beg me not to leave her over the summer? Why did she ask to become our roommate? What was the point of working so hard to make our relationship work if she can sit there and smile hours after it ended? Why am I over here in pain, when I broke up with her?"

I knew exactly what I wanted to say, but I knew the moment didn't call for it. Luckily, Madison came over and suggested the four of us go watch a movie in the basement, relinquishing me of the duty to reply to Xavier in that instant.

January

Down in the fully furnished basement of Madison's family home, Xavier and Amanda were resting on the pullout couch while Madison and I were laying on the blowup mattress behind it. Xavier's questions rang through my mind like a harsh siren. Despite Airplane 2 playing on the television in front of us, and Amanda's boisterous laugh almost supplanting the film's audio, the unrelenting alarm bell grew louder and louder as I looked at my girlfriend and became uneasy. Her body was turned away from me, and she was completely engrossed in the movie she had seen many times before; to the point of ignoring all my advances to cuddle or steal a kiss. I understood she wasn't a lovey-dovey person, but her coldness went beyond that. *How is this the same woman that laid her head on my chest and kissed me so passionately after our first date?* I pondered as the siren reached a deafening pitch. Then, the alarm suddenly died, and a wave of clarity and dejection rolled over me. As we laid there untouching and Madison continued reeling at the movie in tandem with Amanda, it became obvious that I'd been beating a dead horse. Our romance was long dead and on the same path as Xavier and Amanda. The revelation caused me to grow frustrated with each and every guffaw that escaped Madison's lips. Based on the way she had been acting for months, there was no way she was still happy in this sham relationship.

Moments after my own epiphany, I heard Xavier whisper to Amanda the same question that was brewing in my mind. "How can you laugh like that?"

"I just want to make the best of tonight." Amanda replied almost questioningly; clearly bewildered.

Amanda had barely finished her sentence before Xavier let out a booming and sarcastic chortle that nearly shook the basement. Madison twisted her head toward me with her mouth agape and her brow furrowed in confusion, trying to get a hint of what was going on. The tension was so palpable, it seemed as if even the movie itself had come to a hush in order to witness what would happen next.

"That is the dumbest shit I've ever heard." Xavier declared as he yanked the blanket that had been covering him and Amanda, stood up, and wrapped himself with it in a single motion like a superhero donning his cape. Shaken by the outburst, all anyone could do was watch as he stomped up the stairs in a huff.

Amanda looked back at us, her eyes darting between our faces in an attempt to confirm that Xavier's reaction was as unwarranted and startling as she believed.

"What's wrong with him?" Madison asked with a judgmental gaze.

I was in no mood to explain the situation, so I chose to shrug my shoulders as I slid off the air mattress to follow Xavier up the stairs.

Upstairs, Xavier was laying on the living room couch, completely shrouded in darkness. I walked over and sat on the ground in front of the sofa and near his feet. For a few minutes, we stayed just like that; in deep, muted understanding. There wasn't much to say. I already knew the entire situation and how frustrated he had been for over a year. In the end, I just said the first thing on my mind. Trying to lighten the mood and poke fun at his bombastic outburst, I tittered and said "I hate to say it, but after a scene like that I have to. I told you so."

Xavier chuckled and expressed how after two years of dealing with her callous attitude towards their relationship, he just couldn't take it anymore and he exploded. We spent the rest of the night talking about how awkward things would be back home since Amanda and Xavier shared a room, how similar Amanda and Madison were, and, needless to say, the state of my own relationship with Madison.

"You know, I don't know how much longer this thing with Madison is going to last. I shaved my goatee, I ran races, I secretly gave up Special Hookah and my e-hookahs, and I constantly spend money I don't have so I can drive up to see her. I've done everything I can think of to make it work, but it's all in vain if we're both unhappy. I know love is hard sometimes, and you won't be happy in every moment, but I don't think it should feel like a full-time job. I've been stressed like I'm trying to save a broken marriage, and we haven't even known each other for a year. I think we just want different things out of a relationship, and those things aren't meshing. Deep down, I'm sure she feels the same way."

Xavier nodded in agreement and added "We'll both find someone who loves as hard as we do one day man."

"I sure hope you're right." I conceded. "I just hope you know you're stuck with me until I do."

Xavier laughed quietly before responding with a simple "you know it bro."

After a moment of silence I said, "Welp, I'm pooped. I'm assuming you're staying up here for the night, so I'll go update Madison on the sleeping situation so we can all just go to bed. Good night man."

"Good night bro." Xavier replied as I turned my back and started making my way back to the stairs leading to the basement. "Wait!" Xavier whispered as my foot touched down on the first step. As I looked over my shoulder toward his voice, all he said was "when y'all do break up, Special Hookah is coming back with a vengeance."

I couldn't see his face in the darkness, but I knew a huge goofy grin was plastered onto it. I shook my head and laughed while continuing my trek down the stairs.

***

As I finished my stories and the coals burning our proprietary shisha blend had fully turned into ash, that day's session of hookah came to a close. There was nothing left to do but clean up the picnic table we had been using and put everything away so we could head to Pilot House to have our traditional after-smoke meal.

"So how did you and Madison finally end things?" Charles inquired as we broke down the hookah so we could place it inside its bag.

Under the influence and no longer able to tell any story in great detail, I was glad there wasn't much of a tale behind our breakup. Raising my finger to steady myself, I gathered my remaining wits to respond. "A couple days after my birthday, I just asked Madison if she was happy, and she said no. After talking about it, we didn't see our relationship working out, and, not wanting to have things end like it did with Xavier and Amanda, we decided to call it quits." Feeling a tinge of regret, I broke eye-contact with my friends and fell quiet for a moment before nervously laughing and finishing my thought, "It was for the best you know."

Chapter 19

Welcome Home

Deep into the early morning, the clamoring of hammers against cheap plywood driven by exhausted amateur builders rang through the otherwise tranquil night; the occasional expletive expelled out of fatigue-induced frustration joined in the nighttime racket.

"I told you we should have built the beds first." Xavier bemoaned while reading his copy of the directions for the twin bed frames we had gotten for our new apartment. It was the end of a busy afternoon spent in classes, picking up our new mattresses, and transporting most of our belongings from GMU to our new abode located in the basement of a house in Woodbridge, Virginia. It was a humble space; an in-law suite that had its own entrance at the back of the house, a kitchen, and bathroom nicer than anything we had used while living on a college campus.

"Honestly, I thought we'd be better at this," I said while rubbing the back of my head and looking at our mattresses, fresh from the store, standing upright against the wall. "Everything online said it should only take an hour to put together." I looked over at Xavier's progress to see he was at least five steps ahead of me. "Anyway, why are you complaining? You're almost done." I joked.

Xavier snickered and replied without looking up at me. "I can't go to bed with you hammering all night."

"I think I just need a quick break. Then I'll be able to catch up." I retorted as I placed a green apple flavored hookah pen between my lips and stood up. I walked over to a mini blue and white UConn Huskies basketball that was lying in the hallway just beyond the threshold of the tiny room, palming it gently as I picked it up.

"What's up with that ball anyway? I thought you hated basketball?" Xavier jested with a smirk; finally looking up from his half-finished work.

Though I was a bit embarrassed, I recounted the story of how I had won the ball during my 8th-grade graduation trip to Six Flags. Everyone else in my group wanted to ride roller coaster after roller coaster and I could only muster the bravery to tackle two. Once we were in line for the third, feigning a need to use the bathroom, I ran off to the famous and impossible to win theme park games. Wandering from booth to booth while waiting for my friends to finish the ride, I spotted a station with a blue and white ball, stamped with what I thought at the time was a big white wolf, my favorite animal. It was a free throw game and despite my experience earlier that year at Midnight Basketball, I still had some confidence in my free throw abilities. Unfortunately, I didn't win the ball I wanted, but I made enough baskets to win the miniature version; the very one I carried with me into my adulthood.

"When I moved to Virginia in the middle of 9th grade, since I had a hard time making friends for a while, I spent a lot of time juggling this ball in the air, bouncing it up and around like this." I shared as I gave Xavier a demonstration, bouncing the ball off my right forearm to my left wrist and then using my shoulder to bump the ball up once more and off of my head. I finished by catching the ball with my hands. Cringing, I continued my story. "While bouncing this around and listening to music I would escape to an entirely different world similar to the anime and manga that I love. If I liked the scene I had pictured enough, I'd write down the story and attempt to draw it, thinking one day I'd share my epic with the world in a videogame or my own anime," I paused to laugh at myself, "but I had no talent for drawing, so the world of Taradiddle remains a secret in my notebooks."

"Really? So, are you starting to write again?" Xavier asked with a pondering gaze.

"No way" I shot out, laughing so hard at the preposterous idea that the e-hookah I was occasionally puffing fell out of my mouth. "I decided to bring it with me back to Mason after I went home with Madison for Thanksgiving. I thought it might be relaxing to lose myself in music with it sometimes."

"I see. Well, you'll relax even better with a bed if you ever manage to finish." Xavier quipped as he started to get back to work.

Tossing my ball to the side, and feeling a bit competitive, I got back to work with the hope of beating Xavier to the punch.

***

The next day, the morning of March twenty-fifth, 2015, I awoke from my short slumber on my shabbily constructed, but functioning, bed. As the number of days until commencement on May sixteenth waned, the stress of transitioning into adulthood naturally mounted. Yet something about moving into our new home had made our impending future more palpable, pushing me inches away from the line marking the boundary between sanity and a complete meltdown.

Even after months of applying for non-retail, career positions, I had yet to be invited for a single interview. I felt like I had done everything that could be done, but not even my months of free labor in a lab on campus seemed to give me the edge employers were looking for.

At the beginning of the spring semester, I started volunteering in the histology lab at GMU under the guidance of Dr. Esther Peters. I had taken her histology course during the 2014 fall semester and was strangely inspired by the kaleidoscope of colors created by the staining and processing of animal or plant tissue; to the point of offering to help her out in her research. The moment she agreed to let me work under her was one of my proudest moments at Mason, as it meant that I was being recognized by a professor for my potential and that I was on the same successful track as my old roommate, Trey. I was certain that my time in her laboratory combined with my, admittedly minimal, clinical experience at Visionworks would grant me an advantage in the job market. Yet, I was still coming up dry.

Taking a deep sigh as I buried my anxiety for the time being, I got up to get ready for class and noticed Xavier was awake; still lying comfortably in his flawlessly built bed and smiling like a love-struck sap.

"Are you coming back to the apartment tonight, or did you plan on staying at her place again?" I inquired wistfully while getting dressed for the day.

Looking up at the ceiling and raising an eyebrow, he thought for a second before responding with a shrug of his shoulders. "I'm probably going to spend the night over there if Tori lets me." he admitted. Tori was a girl Xavier had started dating a month or so after his breakup with Amanda. I was a bit envious of him since our plan was to enjoy the eligible bachelor life together once I broke up with Madison, but now I spent many nights home alone while he was out gallivanting with Tori.

"Well have fun," I remarked while raising my eyebrows up and down with a sly grin, poking fun at Xavier. Even though I was jealous, it warmed my heart to see how exultant he was laying there in his new bed. "Guess I'll see you tomorrow?" I observed.

"Maybe. Do you work tomorrow?" Xavier asked. Xavier had begun working at Visionworks earlier in the semester as well, and, thanks to the gamut of responsibilities required by my final semester at George Mason, this was where we had sadly begun to spend most of our time together.

"Who knows man, all of the days are melting together at this point" I laughed as I started to make my way out the door. "I'll see-ya when I see-ya, lover boy."

***

Later that morning, I sat in my usual seat in the back row of the lecture hall where classes were held for the hardest course I had ever taken in my college career: Immunology. It was a course I found more difficult than Organic Chemistry and Physics combined, and of course it was the only obstacle standing between myself and graduation. I was able to pull out a B on the first exam, but it was all downhill from there. I quickly fell behind and couldn't seem to grasp the material to the level expected by the professor. This led to me failing the second test, just a hair's breadth away from a D.

As I sat in front of my laptop waiting for the professor to finish setting up, it was clear the first slide of the PowerPoint being projected on the screen was once again beyond my understanding. Exasperated, I relegated myself to sifting through and purging my emails, hoping the tedious and monotonous task would help me to mentally reset and quell my frustrations in order to take the forthcoming lecture with a calm mind that was ready to absorb all of the information like a sponge.

With a dreary look on my face, I supported my head with one hand and scrolled through every old email with the other. Old messages with Dr. Peters, deleted. Old confirmations for economic experiments I participated in for some extra cash, deleted. Receipts from textbook orders, deleted. The act of emptying my inbox was surprisingly satisfying; it was like popping virtual bubble wrap.

Once there was less than a minute left until the class began, I refreshed the web page to see the amount of space I had cleared. For nearly the entire breadth of my college life I hadn't deleted a single email, so it was sure to be gratifying. But then, as the page reloaded, I noticed something; a shining white bar in a sea of grayed out messages. It was a new email at the top of my inbox, and it was from the Fairfax County Health Department.

My heart stopped for a moment, as if holding its breath at the prelude of a race in preparation to unleash a burst of energy the moment the starting horn blared. I clicked the message and shut my eyes immediately. My heart took off. I could feel it beating against my chest rapidly like a child playing with bongos; my mouth felt dry and arid. I took a lone deep and slow breath, before finally opening my eyes.

Gleaming like an oasis in the desert, displayed on my screen was a request for me to come in for an interview. I was so astounded I had nearly forgotten to breathe; only the sound of my professor's voice announcing the start of the lecture pulled me out of the reverie.

I rushed to close my laptop so I could give my full attention, but every thought that crossed my mind as the professor spoke led me back to that email. *Did I imagine the email? There's no way Fairfax County would contact me if no one else did.* I thought as I looked back down at my backpack. *I should open my laptop just to make sure I wasn't daydreaming. No, no I can't do that. I need to pay attention.*

I mulled over whether or not to verify the email's existence for so long, that by the time I convinced myself to do it, the class was being dismissed.

Unable to wait any longer, I snatched my laptop out of my bag as students filed in for the next lecture, pulling up the email and reading it four times over. Each time I read it I believed it less and less, but I knew time was of the essence if I wanted to be one of the first interviewees. I replied with my availability while praying that they could see me the next day; praying that tomorrow would be the day I'd walk through the doors of the Health Department and secure a job with the Disease Carrying Insects Program. It may have only been a seasonal position, but the field work I would be performing with them would be a great learning experience for the future.

After sending my response, I shut my laptop and tossed it back into my bag, finally freeing the seat for a student standing beside me that was visibly irritated by my presence. Avoiding his gaze, I skirted around him and pulled out my phone to share the good news with Xavier as I scurried off gleefully to our old dorm on campus to study up on the position.

When I opened the door to my former home on campus, I was greeted with nothing more than foreboding stillness. Not a soul was present, and the room was strangely dark in spite of the high noon sun outside. A brief sadness touched my soul, like a drop of rain during a sun shower. Hastily, I flipped on the light switch, ousting the shadows that had plagued the dorm. By the time I sat at my desk, I had already shaken the strange dejection that attempted to kill the shining mood I had carried with me to the dorm.

***

The next day, after what felt like a successful interview, I returned to our basement apartment to find the same dispirited emotion washing over me. My heart sank at the sight of another empty dwelling that forced me to realize that the relationships I shared with my friends were changing rapidly. Now that we no longer lived on campus, our daily hangout sessions were becoming scarcer by the day. Charles, having moved off campus before Xavier and myself, had also become more difficult to see. The days of walking over to your buddy's dorm to hang out at a mere whim were gone, and in their place were long commutes through Northern Virginia traffic. Planning around each other's schedules and moods became much more difficult once bills and the other constraints of adulthood were thrown into the mix. My college bubble had popped, and my life was leaking into the real world. For a moment I felt powerless knowing my friends would all be going off in their own directions.

The old adage "out of sight, out of mind" echoed through my brain; it was something I had experienced time and time again while growing up. Each time the military relocated us, regardless of promises made, my friendships would fade into nothingness, and I would never hear from them again. All that remained in the place of my former companionship was a hole I would fill with the first person willing to associate with me in my new neighborhood.

It doesn't have to be that way, I'm not some powerless kid anymore. I silently told myself in an attempt to embolden my spirits. *All I have to do is make more of an effort from here on out.*

I truly believed that. I believed it every time I would pop up at The Gully after classes or work, only to find it empty. I believed it when I would try to make lunch plans with someone and one of us would be forced to cancel because of an assignment for class or a job interview. I believed it every time I came home to an empty and dark apartment.

This belief I held deep in my soul acted as a shield from the gloom that emanated from the ever-darkening shadows in our apartment. That is, until the day Charles told me that he would be moving to China for a teaching opportunity. On that day, as I congratulated him on the job and cracked a smile, I felt a crack form in the shield. No matter how hard I tried, life could pull us apart. If Charles left for China, he was sure to forget about a nobody like myself. He had so many wild and adventurous friends, and he was certainly going to make even more in China. There was no doubt in my mind I would fade into a vague memory. I realized how small I was and began to perceive my efforts as irrelevant. *This must be fate.* I surmised.

As the semester rolled on, the darkness slowly trickled through the crack and took root in the fertile soil of my cavernous soul, undeterred by the good happenings around me. A promotion at Visionworks, being offered the job with the DCIP, and even passing my third Immunology exam well enough to bring my grade back up to a C, it all did little more than put a smile on my face that was quickly wiped away by the darkness whispering from its new den.

"Good for you! more hours to add to your busy schedule."

"Congratulations on securing a temporary position! Maybe next time you'll get a real job."

"Oh, look at that. If you get anything less than a C on the final exam you'll fail the class."

I felt so desperate to escape the taunting whispers, that I begged Madison to take me back in any capacity. I didn't care if we started dating again, or if we just became friends with benefits. I just needed whatever relief she could provide from whatever was gnawing at my soul. Of course, most likely creeped out by the desperation, she rejected me again and again, widening the crack each time and granting the shadows greater access to the pit in my heart.

Soon, even my usual means of worldly escape ceased to work. I couldn't find pleasure in my videogames, and anime seemed to lose its flair. The only tools left on my belt that could handle the job of relaxing my mind were my hookah pens and UConn Huskies ball. Thankfully, they were up to the task; chain smoking the pens and dribbling the ball in the air while listening to Motion City Soundtrack carried me through to the end of the semester. The battles, the tragedies, and the twists I would invent for the imaginary denizens of Taradiddle helped me to forget the ones in my own life.

The week of my graduation, my family came to visit and witness the momentous occasion. Seeing my brother,

Selvon, in particular, provided a much-needed reprieve from the melancholy that had ruled my life for over a month. Xavier also joined us in the celebrations and watched me walk across the stage during convocation for the College of Science on May thirteenth, meshing so well with my family that my mom declared him her son from another mother.

Three days later, on the day of commencement (the university-wide graduation ceremony), we decided to skip the proceedings and spend the few remaining hours with my family eating out and having a huge breakfast. Why waste time sitting quietly for two hours while surrounded by strangers, when we could stuff our faces silly and jubilate in a nearly empty restaurant before anyone else could arrive?

After the upbeat and festive meal, my family hauled themselves into the car as quickly as ever and my dad pulled off in a hurry. I was sad to watch them leave, but eager to return home with Xavier to the bottles of liquor waiting for us on our pool table back home. We drank all day and into the night, topping the celebrations off by smoking hookah on the backyard walkway that led to our door. "So how does it feel?" Xavier inquired while taking a drag from the hose, seeking a sneak peek at his future since there was still one more semester standing between him and his own graduation.

"Scary as hell." I expressed with a chuckle. "I'm starting a new position on Monday, I'll still be working at Visionworks part-time in case I can't find another full-time job before the season is over, and I'll still be volunteering in Dr. Peter's lab a few days a week. I just hope I can handle it."

Grimacing at the heavy workload, Xavier responded by handing me the hose. "Well just enjoy the night before you stress about all of that."

I grabbed the hose and pulled slowly, allowing the clouds of burnt tobacco to warm my lungs and soul. "You're right man," I admitted, blowing the white clouds out of my nose, "today's not the day for that."

Still, I couldn't shake the feeling that had taken up residence inside of me.

"**This won't last**" it murmured from its burrow in my soul. "**It never lasts.**"

Chapter 20

The Infernal Mirror

On a dark night during the final days of June, A Gabriel Iglesias comedy special played on my laptop as I sat alone on the floor gazing at the screen, hoping to laugh. The wry and desperate look on my face intensified with each joke that failed to hit my funny bone. I had watched the special before, and knew I found it hilarious, but for some reason not even a chuckle slipped out of me. Drunk as I was, it should have been all the easier to throw me into a fit of laughter, yet I couldn't even force a smile onto my face as the comedian sputtered off punchlines accompanied by perfectly executed, a cappella sound effects. *Am I broken?* I pondered as I sat up and closed my laptop, giving up on happiness for the night.

Working for the Disease Carrying Insects Program was the most enjoyable and fruitful position I had ever had the pleasure of undertaking. Through the daily grind of placing and picking up mosquito and tick traps, I gained a love for the field work involved in monitoring and research. Travelling to the furthest reaches of Fairfax County under the punishing sun while behind the wheel of a pickup truck was a welcome change from the procedures of the histology lab I still volunteered in, and the pseudo-clinical environment of Visionworks. Every day opened new possibilities, bringing with it some form of chaos that could throw us for a loop; from a large black snake blocking the path to a trap, to a truck nearly rolling down a cliff on a narrow hillside road.

More so than the actual work though, my colleagues were what made me excited to get up every single weekday. A cast of joyful and compassionate characters that reminded me of my days back in Eisenhower when the crew and I would shoot the breeze throughout the night. Only now the comfort of a couch at midnight was replaced by a hot pickup under the high noon sun.

Within DCIP, only five of us were seasonal hires that handled most of the setup and pickup for the traps. First there was Rich, the hyper confident and affable, alpha male of the group. Then there was Sam, an incredibly intelligent and highly driven individual that seemed ironically plagued with the physical clumsiness of an air-headed bimbo. Next there was Cas, the only woman within our group and a goofy, amateur astrologer with curly hair that believed all the answers could be found in the stars. Oddly enough, and to her credit, her predictions and books were often right; almost to the point of making me believe in astrology myself.

Lastly there was Pedro. An artist who, during our first conversation, called me a "dumbass," but would later grow to become my greatest friend within DCIP. He was a bit awkward when it came to meeting new people, hence the name-calling he hoped I would realize was a joke, but he had a heart of gold that he wore on his sleeve. He was the youngest employee within DCIP, and in fact the only one younger than myself. Since we also shared a similar dark and quirky sense of humor, we got along quite well. He helped me to feel at home amongst my older peers during my first month in the department.

Sadly, no matter how kind and welcoming my colleagues were, I couldn't open up to them; my instincts screamed not to let them in. Keeping my coworkers at arm's length meant they could never be snatched from me, and I would never have to experience that pain again. Each day, as I sat in my car after a long day of bug catching, I abandoned the light granted to me by their positivity, and submitted myself to the dark and persistent feeling that would haunt me through the solitude of my commute and surely follow me into my empty home if I was so unfortunate as to have a day off from the histology lab at GMU.

Every moment I was alone, I'd feel an inescapable stream of negativity leak from the cavern within me. So, with Xavier's presence at home becoming scarcer as he opted to spend most days and nights with Tori, work became my only relief. The stress and exhaustion caused by constant work, though rough on my body, also allowed me a daily modicum of mental and spiritual peace by making me so tired that I was impelled to turn in for the night as soon as I walked through the sliding glass doors of my apartment.

The shadows within the emptiness grew more and more ravenous by the day, exponentially so during the odd weekend where I wasn't on the schedule at Visionworks and had nothing else to do but wallow in my own mind. I spent most of this time bouncing my blue and white ball around the basement I called home while jamming to my favorite tunes, thrusting myself into the world of Taradiddle to keep the voracious darkness in my spirit at bay. Then one day, out of the blue, the magic that once emanated from the combination of my dingy ball and hyped-up music died.

No matter how much I tossed the ball around, and no matter how beautiful or inspiring a song was, I couldn't picture a thing. It was as if my imagination itself had been consumed by the ever-growing umbra in my core that refused to be ignored. The only comfort I had left was my pack of disposable hookah pens I had begun to ration since the item appeared to have been discontinued. No matter how hard I searched, I could no longer find the brand I had been smoking for years, and thus I had no choice but to make my supply last as long as possible. Of course, rationing didn't serve to quell my starving soul, nor the parasite that had grown too large for its burrow, so I started smoking from the full-sized hookah on my own, and what was once a communal experience where stories and laughs were shared, had been reduced to a daily depressive meditation.

Eventually, even that wasn't enough to stave off the black tendrils that were now binding and strangling my soul, so I turned to the internet to search for easy companionship and found an attractive blonde that seemed nearly as desperate as myself. I had thought that maybe my luck was turning for the better after our first date. She had decided to spend the night, and the next day I excitedly explained to Xavier how my age-old method for initiating a first kiss had worked again. I believed that I had found my "Tori". That is, of course, until I felt a tingle in my throat that, within a day, grew into a stinging pain that prevented me from swallowing.

After a round of antibiotics, I was physically back to normal around the middle of June, but the mental damage remained. It felt as if God himself had punished me for my floozy behavior, and I couldn't bring myself to try online dating again. The dregs of my will to fight against fate were finally exhausted, and I accepted my curse to die alone.

With that resignation, it felt like I had finally become one with the whispering force within me. Everything I did throughout the remaining half of June felt empty. Even at my jobs that had once been my sanctuaries, the numbness never subsided. I was still capable of putting on a happy and professional mask for my coworkers, but quickly this began to eat at me as well. I came to secretly resent the happiness of those around me, and the jovial and friendly attitudes of my colleagues were especially vexing. Wearing that facade nearly every day caused me to even lash out at Xavier, the few times I had gotten to see him, out of envy. I would refuse to go out with him if Tori was involved in any way, wanting nothing less than to be around the woman I had come to believe was stealing my best friend. In my mind, sitting on my floor and drinking myself into a stupor was a much more attractive option than watching the person who was supposed to stick by my side through everything, instead leave me just like the rest.

Everything came to a head at the end of the month as I was clocking out from my usual Sunday shift at Visionworks. I overheard a patient say "Ain't nothing better than waking up to another twenty-four," and my customer-service smile melted away as a look of disgust replaced it. I walked out the door as quickly as I could, wondering how anyone could say that with a straight face. *What's so great about living when we all die in the end anyway? Every new twenty-four is just another chance to suffer.* I mentally rebutted. *The sooner you die, the sooner the pain ends.*

Once I sat in my car, I was beside myself due to my own knee-jerk reaction to someone simply appreciating life itself. *Why can't I be as carefree and appreciative as him?* I wondered. I chewed over the question for the entire duration of my commute home, and by the time I entered my neighborhood, the answer was obvious. My life felt pointless. I had no passions in this world beyond my friends and family, and therefore no personal goals or dreams of my own. College had blessed me with an array of distractions along with scholastic and professional objectives to strive for that allowed me to ignore this deep-seeded issue, and instead of wisely using my time in university to determine who I truly was and what I wanted to accomplish in life, I just followed the path laid out by the status quo: get good grades, intern for experience, and choose a career path that pays well and will always be needed in society.

I supposed the family I had always dreamt of could have given me the reason to live that I sought, but I couldn't give myself a single rationale for my life-long desire beyond my fear of loneliness. *Did I only want to have a family so I could surround myself with people that were forced to love me and keep me company?* I wondered. "That shouldn't be the only reason to have a family." I murmured to myself between my teeth. "One should start a family out of love, not fear."

Finally parking in front of our home, and on the brink of losing myself, my eyes welled up with tears once I noticed Xavier's car was nowhere to be seen once again. I needed someone to talk to. Anyone. I scrolled through the contacts on my phone, desperate for a shoulder to cry on, and the only person that seemed capable of lightening my load, was my mother.

I called her, and she answered quickly as always with a loud and extended "Tre!"; the nickname given to me since I was the third Anthony S. Drayton in the family. The unconditional love in her voice caused my own to crack as I greeted her back, betraying my descent into despair.

Without skipping a beat, she asked me if I was okay, and, unable to hold back my anguish any longer, I whimpered "no mom, things have been really hard." I told her about how distant I felt from my friends now that we were off campus. I divulged to her that I didn't feel like I had a purpose. I even admitted that dating felt impossible and that I couldn't imagine finding anyone that would love me.

Out of character, she let me speak without interrupting, only making the occasional noise to signal that she was still listening. Once I had finished voicing my woes, the heartbreak in my mother's voice was evident. Unfortunately, she didn't have much advice for me, only being able to tell me that I would always be loved by my family at home and that if things became too difficult for me to cope with, I could always move down to South Carolina with them.

While I appreciated the assurance that I always would have a loving home, her words were not what I wanted to hear. Turning tail and running back to mommy was a sign of failure; a sign that I couldn't hack it on my own. If I failed to do something so simple, it would confirm my worthlessness.

"**But maybe you can't do this?**", the imp on my shoulder reasoned, "**It's not like there is anything special about you. Maybe you should just give up.**"

I told my mom I'd think about it, and she reassured me once again, before hanging up, that I always had a place at her and my father's house. After the call ended, I sat in my car for a minute, sobbing and weighing my options. I hated the idea of becoming a quitter, but the more I ruminated on the alleviation that life at my parents' house would bring, the more tempting it became.

"This is too much to think about right now. I should just go to sleep." I told myself as I exited my car and headed inside, hoping a good night's rest would bring me the answer I desired. I rushed inside and tossed myself in bed. I felt too lethargic and crestfallen to even remove the dress clothes that I had worn to work. I looked down at the purple tie around my throat that had served as part of my pledge uniform nearly three years ago. *If only I could go back to those days.* I mused as I fell asleep.

Hours later, as the early morning sun peeked through the blinds of my window, I awoke in a daze and still wearing my work clothes from the night before. My mind felt hazy. It was as if my body was on autopilot and I was nothing more than a passenger forced to peer through my own eyes as I got up and left, without so much as brushing my teeth, for another shift peddling eyeglasses and performing pretests for the doctor. I felt devoid of emotion the entire day. There was no sadness or happiness. I didn't feel the slightest tint of anger or hope. I was simply a machine, functioning as designed until my shift ended.

Yesterday I was so distraught that I couldn't stop crying while I was on the phone with my mother, and now nothing. Will I feel this way for the rest of my life? I contemplated.

The minute I got home that afternoon, I sauntered over to the bathroom. I placed my hands on the side of the sink and leaned over, staring myself in the eyes and imagining the saddest scenarios life could throw at me. My intention was to bring myself to tears and prove I hadn't finally snapped, but no matter what I came up with, whether it was the death of our family dog or my parents disowning me, there wasn't a single drop.

I looked down at the sink, closing my eyes and accepting the results of my little experiment. *I guess this is what it feels like when you finally internalize it.* I theorized. *When you finally give up and accept that..*

"You are alone."

Interjected a mocking and cackling voice.

My eyes shot open, and I held my breath. The voice seemed to resonate from every direction around me, and clearly didn't belong to my absent roommate. Oddly enough, I wasn't afraid. I was simply shocked by the sudden voice that announced the presence of a stranger in my home.

I stood up straight and slowly spun around in order to locate the intruder, but my surroundings were clear. *I really am losing it.* I mentally proclaimed to myself while turning back to the mirror, instinctively jumping two steps back as I was greeted by my reflection grinning back at me. Its smile grew wider, seemingly out of glee as it twirled its own purple tie that hung from its neck and exposed rows of knife-like fangs.

I looked askance at what used to be my reflection, unable to pry my gaze away from those damned teeth poking out from between the lips of my doppelganger. For the first time all day, I felt an emotion: Anger.

Chapter 21

Stepping Forward

Pointing at me with his free hand while twirling the glimmering violet cloth around his neck, the doppelganger was barely capable of muttering "**Look at the state of you!**" between fits of laughter that intensified with each word.

I clenched my fist so tightly out of frustration it began to shake, and I started to cut my eyes at the irreverent creature that was housed within the mirror. I stuck my hands in my pocket in an attempt to calm myself. Then I grumbled the only question on my mind: "What do you want?"

The menace of the mirror stopped twirling his tie the moment the query left my lips, adopting a curious position by supporting his head with one hand before replying "**I wonder what choice you'll make this time**." The glee in his voice was present in every breath he took. He gestured downward toward my feet, directing my gaze at what laid beneath me. But I already knew what came next, so there was no need for me to look down at the all-consuming blackhole that formed underneath me, slowly dragging me into its depths. I considered what followed as inevitable and didn't bother struggling against the pull of the shadows.

My hands remained planted in my pockets as I leered, unblinking, at the doppelganger that seemed to revel at the scene, looking down on me as I sank into the abyss. The last thing I heard spewed from those infernal lips, before the shadows blackened my vision, was "**See you soon**."

After a few seconds had passed, the blackness cleared from my vision like fog at dawn, and I could see the decrepit old witch standing atop the same towering crag that pointed toward the exit of the cave.

"No facade to lure me in this time, huh?" I scoffed as my anger began to dissipate, knowing the dream would soon be over. A tinge of fear entered my heart as I mentally prepared for the same choice that always shook my soul so intensely that my body ripped me back to reality in self-defense. But something was off; this emotion, normally composed of pure fear, was tainted by drop of puzzlement.

While watching the witch stand on the peak before me, as the wind caused her tattered violet dress to flutter and her long, olive-green curls to dance wildly, I noticed something looked different about her. Her face appeared bored.

Normally, this was the point in time where she would walk toward me while speaking in a voice only my spirit understood, but instead the only steps I heard came from behind me. The footsteps stopped to my right, and I swung my head quickly to determine what it could be. Standing beside me, appearing quite smug and with arms crossed, was the doppelganger from my mirror.

I gripped my thighs through the fabric in my pockets to maintain my composure. My jaw fell to the ground out of confusion and disbelief. *There's never been someone else here before. What is going on?*

The doppelganger nodded in the direction of the old hag standing on the rock, as if signaling his task had been completed. In turn, she started to strut down the slope, forming the familiar shapes in her palms that I had never been able to make out. Terror filled my being as inaudible words that caused my soul itself to shiver began to pour from between her menacing maw. I could feel myself fading as I always had at this point; my brain ejecting me back into the waking world. I closed my eyes to welcome the quick escape.

Then I heard something. It was so quick I almost believed I hadn't heard anything at all. I turned to my right once more and opened my eyes; the disappointed face of the doppelganger confirmed my suspicions. He had called me pathetic.

Suddenly, irritation bubbled up within me. Terrorizing me was no longer enough for this grey-skinned crone and her new lackey. Her frown of tedium, and the doppelganger's comment made it feel as if I were simply a broken toy. As if my constant running away from the options before me caused them both to grow tired of this little game.

My mind went wild. *What gives them the right to haunt me? What gives them a right to demand an answer from me? I don't know who she is, where she comes from, or why she chose me, yet she's bored as if I asked for this?* I pulled my hands out of my pocket with my fists balled before declaring my resolve in my head. *I refuse to be toyed with anymore!* I was tired of running. I was tired of this nightmare. I was tired of waking up drenched in sweat and out of breath.

As the witch came to a halt only a few feet away from me, I took a forceful step forward in an act of defiance, intending to finally respond to her for the first time in my life. Then, as my lips parted to yell the first word in my tirade to refuse ever giving her what she wanted, my vision became cloudy, and I collapsed onto my knees, narrowly preventing my face from slamming against the cave floor by catching myself with my left hand. My limbs felt wobbly, and my body became feeble. I palmed my face with my right hand as if squeezing my head would remove the haze and weakness that had overcome me.

I looked up at the witch through the gaps in my fingers, and while I couldn't quite see her face thanks to her towering figure, I saw the smokey shapes she once held dissipate into nothingness. My vision became even more blurred as the cave started to fade from existence around me in all directions, moving from the outer walls inward. My brain was scrambled, and I couldn't form a single thought, but, before the cave of nightmares finally disappeared, I couldn't help but catch the faint but undoubtedly pleased smirk on the face of my doppelganger as he was erased along with our surroundings. It was as if my would-be riposte was exactly what he sought.

For what felt like an hour, my consciousness floated in nothingness. I couldn't see a single thing, but it wasn't the same as when I had been blinded by shadows in the past. It was peaceful; almost like sitting in the deepest corner of a steam room and allowing the vapors to obscure everything before me as they warmed and enveloped the body I couldn't feel.

Suddenly, I could sense a wall behind me, and my center of gravity seemed to shift. The sensation of my limbs returned, and I could feel that I was lying down on my back. I became aware of my eyelids once again, and in turn I started to open them slowly.

I was back in my bed and still wearing my clothes from my shift at the optometrist. I looked at my phone to confirm my theory and started to smile from ear to ear as my screen lit up. It was 5:00a.m. Monday morning. *I guess that whole day was a dream.* I deduced.

I scanned my left hand as I opened and closed it repeatedly. I felt as if a weight had been lifted off my shoulders; like the dark beast that had claimed the cavern had finally been slain. I had won and I would never see that witch again. Deep in my bones I knew it.

I didn't know what I had done, but I felt emboldened. If I could put an end to that terror, I could do anything. Even refill the now vacant hollow in which it once resided, which now cried to be filled once more.

***

I knew the first step I needed to take was removing myself from the overbearing loneliness in the basement, so that Thursday I finally agreed to go out for drinks with Cas and Sam, who had been wanting to drag everyone to this fancy bar Sam had visited in D.C. once before. It didn't take much convincing for Rich to include himself in the outing, and Pedro, though still too young to drink, decided to join us as well after seeing that and I was finally willing to go out with the team. As much as I hated moving about the crowds of tourists that frequented the streets of the capital of the United States by day and the horde of clubbers and drunks that filled it by night, I knew it was a necessary evil. I did invite Xavier in order to make the experience more comfortable for me, but he swiftly declined since it was a workday and he needed to help Tori with some errands. Disappointed but not dismayed, I still went along with the after-work soiree in the upscale hotel bar.

At first it was pretty awkward, given that I couldn't afford much liquid courage with the cheapest drink being priced at $15, but eventually I found my footing while joking with Rich and Pedro about being the poorest people in the room and fawning with Sam over Cas' unapproachably attractive friends that she had roped in at the last minute.

The night turned out to be surprisingly delightful and convivial, though painfully sober, and I was proud of my accomplishment. Excluding some dates with Madison, it had been years since I had engaged in any form of merriment or gratification that didn't involve either Xavier or Charles. That night proved to me that I could start a social life that didn't depend on them. It meant that once I had faded into the background of their lives, never to be acknowledged again, I would be able to stand on my own two feet.

The very next day, while waiting for Pedro to set up a mosquito trap at one of the collection sites, I received a text from Charles that left me befuddled. I hadn't seen him since graduation, and only a month remained until he would be leaving the country. *What could he want?* I wondered as I opened the message.

What I read left me giddy as a child on Christmas; he was asking if I wanted to go out to a hookah bar with him and a couple of Eunice's friends that night. I couldn't believe it, he wanted to share some of his quickly dwindling time in the states with me.

I felt slightly apprehensive, knowing Eunice would certainly be making an appearance that night; the mere memories of my efforts to woo her in the past were more than enough to make me cringe. *Then again, I can't embarrass myself any more around her than I have in the past. And maybe she has some cute friends. I could certainly use some practice flirting.* I pondered while convincing myself the night out was worth the risk. *And how could I ignore the siren call of gooey shisha?*

Thinking this would be a great opportunity to get the proverbial band back together, I asked Xavier if he would like to join us. Alas, unlike myself, he denied the hookah's cry, claiming he wasn't in the mood for going out to a hookah bar.

What is his problem? I wondered as I stared at his message of declination in disbelief. It felt as if he had lost all interest in everything that had brought us together in the first place. I squeezed my phone out of bitterness. *I don't need him anyway.* I proclaimed to myself while throwing my phone in my pocket and sitting back down in the driver seat of the truck as Pedro returned to the vehicle.

Later that evening, I arrived at the hookah bar casually dressed to the nines, wearing my new black and golden Armani Exchange watch and my navy blue mid top Ralph Lauren shoes; I was ready to seduce one of Eunice's friends. The plan was simple: chat up whichever woman caught my eye first and draw smoke from the hose whenever I couldn't think of anything to continue the conversation.

As I stepped through the threshold of the door, I quickly noticed Charles sitting next to the bombshell that was the object of my affection in years past. A couple of Charles' and Eunice's friends that I had seen on several occasions encircled the table where two hookahs were being set up. I waved over at Charles, and he gestured me over while yelling "Yo!" over the music that boomed from the speakers of the venue. I started to make my way over while looking at all the familiar faces bordering the table, pausing only for a moment as I noticed an unfamiliar angel with shoulder length black hair and red lipstick seated directly across from Eunice. Suddenly, my hands were sweaty, and it was like my mouth was full of peanut butter. A prepubescent squeak accompanied my greeting to the table, and I could feel drops of sweat start to form on my forehead out of nervousness.

Upon taking my seat, all of the ladies took to the dance floor, and I seized my opportunity to ask Charles who the mysterious enchantress was. He wasn't sure and told me that all he knew was that her name was Angie and that Eunice had met her at a job interview earlier that day. For the rest of the night, I was completely captivated by the femme fatale whose deathly beauty itself was so intoxicating I was unable to form a single intelligible word around her. Talking to Eunice was a cake walk in comparison.

At the end of the night when our group stood outside the hookah bar as everyone said their goodbyes, I realized that I was wasting what may have been my one and only chance to ask her on a date since she was only out with us after a chance encounter with Eunice. I did my best to muster up the courage to ask for her number but gave up under the self-imposed pressure. Unable to imagine a single scenario that ended in my favor, I accepted my certain defeat at the hands of such an angel that shone too bright and started to walk off to my car.

But just before I stepped off the curb, I felt a tap on my shoulder and jerked out of surprise. I turned around cautiously and standing before me was the beauty in red lipstick with her phone in her hands. "Before you go, I was trying to add everyone on Facebook. I'm staying with my brother in the area for the summer and it'd be nice to have some friends around here." she divulged with a cute angelic smile. I stood in stunned silence for a second, trying to remember my own name before the quiet became awkward. As a cheesy smile crossed my face, I pointed at her screen to help find my profile.

"Yep that's me, Anthony Drayton." I said once we finally found it.

"Hope we can hang out again sometime!" she sang after sending the friend request. I waved goodbye and reciprocated her smile with an oafish grin, scurrying off to my car before I could tarnish her perception of me.

That very same night, after finally lying down in my bed, I decided to send her a message, telling her that I thought she was cute and that I'd love to see her again sooner than later.

Best to strike while the iron's hot. I asserted to myself as I laid there and awaited her reply. *I can't let a little fear of rejection hold me back anymore.*

While dozing off, the night's events ran through my mind like a clip show. *Hookah, friends, and a mystery girl. What more could a guy want?* I thought while scrolling through my phone mindlessly. Suddenly, the flavor of my mouth turned sour with rancor and my face instantly became grim as Xavier came to mind.

Chapter 22

Love

By the end of July, I was completely overpowered by the enchanting spell cast by a restaurant that Pedro had discovered; a little ramen joint that had recently opened up in Fairfax, Virginia. I had passed it several times without noticing, since it was hidden and overshadowed by its larger neighbors, but Pedro recommended this gem during one of our weekly happy-hour outings with the DCIP crew, and I fell in love the moment I took a slurp of my first authentic bowl. The tender chashu that melted the instant it touched my tongue, the provocatively flavorsome broth, and perfectly cooked noodles became my drug. I couldn't help but constantly invite everyone I knew to that culinary paradise in order to feed my addiction, and before he could escape to China, I had Charles join me for a farewell meal at this brothy promised land.

We spent the entire early dinner reminiscing about how we met in that common room way back when, and the endless nights we had spent playing chess and watching late night cartoons about a talking rump on legs that happened to be a hardened cop that didn't play by the rules. We poked fun at each other's old crushes and our failures at making them our beau, and we chortled at our many drunken escapades around Mason. For two hours, our memories and nostalgia flooded the empty restaurant as the staff shuffled around and prepared for the dinner rush.

Once more patrons started entering the restaurant, we decided it was time to head out and we said our goodbyes. I dapped Charles up and we hugged as I wished him good luck with teaching in China. "Thanks for nearly driving me to insanity with your constant and frustrating lessons," I joked while turning away and heading toward my car, yelling to him that he was going to do great things in China. "Hopefully, you'll be able to teach me some more when you come back in a year," I added solemnly.

Charles laughed boisterously, knowing full well that our frequent debates often left me defeated and feeling uneducated in comparison. "Hey man, you've gotten better at arguing since Eisenhower."

"All thanks to you," I retorted instantly, raising my eyebrows in jest while chuckling.

As we reached our car doors, we each gave a final wave to the other and yelled "Later man!"

For a minute, I sat in my car with misty eyes. This time, unlike the last, the cause was a mix of emotions ranging from happiness to have ever known such a wholesome person, and sorrow from knowing I would probably never see him again.

"Goodbye Charles." I mumbled to myself while watching him drive away in his car and starting the ignition of my own.

***

In spite of the fact that I was getting out of the house a bit more and getting back into the dating game, I could still hear the pit in my core crying to be replenished. Conquering one of my deepest fears seemed to have eradicated the taunting shadows, but every bright moment of my life was stained with a tinge of grey worry that one day they would return more formidable than ever before. Until the moment something else staked claim to its land, the threat would loom over me. Worse yet, anything could trigger the regression.

That is why, a few days after Charles' departure, I was vexed at the sight of Xavier returning home from a weeks-long stay at Tori's place. I was sitting on the futon and playing video games, immersed in an adventure to find the wicked and mystical jester that had cursed my king. I nearly fell out of my seat thanks to the shocking squeak that sprung from the glass door to our apartment as it slid open. I cut my eyes as I watched him step inside, shutting the door and closing the blinds behind him. While he took off his shoes, I couldn't help but feel annoyed after being shaken from my trance so abruptly and I felt keen to show it. I gestured towards his feet with a mocking face. "Planning to stay for a while? I almost forgot you lived here." I asserted.

He squinted both of his eyes, obviously reading the undertones of my statement, and cleared his throat before responding calmly. "Yeah I thought I'd come hang with my boy for a night," he gaily proclaimed.

"Oh, I see, I feel so special!" I said while sarcastically placing my hand over my heart and dropping my jaw to appear touched at the thought.

With an exasperated sigh that signaled he had finally reached his tipping point, he demanded to know what my problem was as he ambled over with a resolute yet confused look in his eyes. "Lately, it's like no matter what I say or do you get angry." he stated, his voice shaky in an attempt to hold back his desire to yell.

I was taken aback. Xavier was never one to confront someone directly. He was always the person trying to deescalate a situation. The only times I had ever seen him this irate was the day he had broken up with Amanda, or the hours that followed the moment our former fraternal president's hands were torn from his throat. Even in those situations he had chosen to remove himself from the irritant or his aggressor. Yet here he was, walking toward me and pushing for answers.

I looked away from him and turned my attention back to the tv screen in front of me, pretending to play my game by randomly moving my character around the screen. "Maybe if you were around like you said you would be, I wouldn't always have a problem with the things you said." I suggested as I felt a headache emerge from my rising ire.

"Like I said I would be? What are you talking about? You are the one who refuses to spend time with me when Tori is around. All you want to do is go out and party when you know I'd rather stay at home and relax." he stated firmly, but not raising his voice in the slightest.

I tossed the orange and grey controller I had been playing with onto the minimalist black coffee table in front of me with so much force that it slid right off and onto the floor with a loud clack. "I don't want to spend time with her because you are always with her and her kid! I'm sorry if that isn't exactly appealing to a twenty-two-year-old man that has been spending the vast majority of his time alone in his apartment. I want to spend time with my best friend doing what we used to do in college just a couple months ago, but I've become too boring for him."

Xavier appeared flabbergasted at my accusations, "You're the boring one?" He questioned, "I feel like the boring one! You treat Tori and me like we have the plague when we invite you over her place. You act like you and I didn't spend most days in our dorm, binging horror movies or watching tv. Like all we did was drink and smoke!" He added fervently.

I clenched my jaw before turning to him and admitting my true feelings. "How many times do I have to say it? I just want to hang out with you; just us guys. I want to tell you about my date with Angie and how she laughed me off when she found out I was five years younger than her. I want to tell you about how I had to call my mom and cry because I couldn't handle being a real adult. I want to tell you that no matter how motivated I am to lead a successful life, sometimes it just feels pointless. I feel worthless. No one will love me, I will never find a reason to exist, and I will die alone; at best, I am an enjoyable blip in the footnotes of someone else's life. So, I'm sorry if the thought of holding all that in while sitting with a happy couple makes me sick."

Xavier's face softened as he took in my words, and for a moment he seemed to pity me. "Look, maybe I have been absent, but that's life. This is what it would be like if I married Tori. I wouldn't be able to see you every day. It's just a fact of life that as we get older, we'll see each other less." He dithered for a moment, knowing his next words may be the most important ones ever spoken in our friendship. "I love you man, and I will be there for you. Sometimes I may not be able to be there for you physically, but you'll always have my support. We have to learn to enjoy every moment we can manage to be together, but also learn to be okay when we can't be," A soft grin crossed his face and he concluded by saying "and unless you tell me you want to stop being friends, you're not getting rid of me. We're brothers."

With those words, my heart began to burn like shimmering embers in a hearth of bliss, bringing light to my once ill-lit cavern. The embers grew into roaring flames that bathed the void in its entirety. The emptiness that bedeviled me for five months was satiated with a simple monologue from Xavier, and I was ashamed.

That blinding joy was artificial; its existence born from the brief expression of love and friendship. I already knew that Xavier was my brother in every way but blood, I shouldn't have needed his reassurance in order to feel like I was worth something. The fact that it took so little to tip the emotional scale in my favor felt sickening, but it provided me with an epiphany.

"You know," I said looking down at the carpet of our basement home, "I think I've always been like this. It happened with Amber. It happened with Madison. It happened briefly when I thought I'd be kicked out of our pledge class during the debacle about the Holocaust Museum. I just can't seem to function unless someone is actively showing me that they care." I took a breath before continuing, coming to grips with what felt like a breakthrough into my own psyche, "I love you too man, just as much as my own brother. I already knew that you'd always be there for me, but for some reason I couldn't escape the feeling that no one except for my immediate family loved me. Myself included.

Xavier remained unblinking, staring at my face and listening intently to what I had to say, only nodding occasionally so I knew he was listening.

"I always viewed myself as a completely uninteresting piece of trash without a purpose. I always believed everyone I knew was ready to get rid of me the second I was no longer convenient. It led me to becoming a desperate beggar of affection that became a train-wreck when I felt that love disappearing."

I sat silently in search of the words that explained my storm of thoughts and emotions, and Xavier took that moment to chime in. "I know the feeling man. My entire relationship with Amanda I felt like there wasn't anyone that would treat me better than her; that she was the best I could ever have.

So, I did everything I could to keep her. Still, you kept pushing and pushing. Telling me I deserve someone that would love me as hard as I loved them. Someone I was actually compatible with, and no longer settling for. Someone that inspired me to improve because of who they are, not because I wanted to keep their interest in me." Xavier tittered under his breath, "but it seems like you didn't believe that for yourself."

I laughed at his astute observation, "You're right about that. I have always known you were a good and passionate person that deserved the best this world had to offer; ever since the moment you rushed in front to protect me from The President without a moment of hesitation. The day we met you told me that even though you were unable to join the Coast Guard, your goal was to find a career that would allow you to help others in any way you could, and in that moment you proved it."

"You don't have to throw yourself in front of someone's attacker to be worthy of finding love," he argued.

I looked at him and smiled gently and giggled, "You're right, I guess I was just a little biased after you saved my ass. But I think my problem is that, unlike you, I've been searching for someone to love me, rather than someone to share my love with. I've been selfishly trying to fill a hole inside of me with love from outside sources, as proof of my worth, but I realize now that I'll never be able to lead a happy-fulfilling life unless I fill it on my own. I have to learn to love myself."

"So, what are you going to do about it?" he inquired while leaning in as if he were about to hear the secret to life.

"Who knows?" I answered with a smirk and stroking my goatee, basking in the glow of what would be the most difficult challenge of my life. "Even though I know what the problem is, there aren't exactly any instructions on how to fix it. The only thing I know is that I can't give up if I ever want to stop feeling like I do now." I got up from my seat to collect the controller that had fallen on the floor and continued to the bookshelf that sat beneath the tv on the wall, picking up a second controller. "I think the first thing I need to do is get over my own ego and start hanging out with my best friend and his new family from time to time. I'm sorry for how I've been acting these past few months man, thanks for being patient with me."

"Of course," he responded with a huge smile that left all of his teeth on display.

As we spent the night shooting zombies until our hands cramped, I was in a state beyond happiness and melancholy. It was a state that would take me years to enter by my lonesome, and one that would require a voyage across uncharted seas to master; seas blessed by a sparkling sun but tormented with nights darker than I had ever sailed through before. It was a feeling that didn't rely on momentary joy, and it didn't wallow in temporary sadness. It allowed me to enjoy the moment, fully aware of the rough, boundless, journey of self-discovery that would begin the next day. For the first time in my life, I was okay.

Chapter 23

Go and Commit This to Memory

"Like hell I'm paying extra for six people at an empty bar" Xavier yelled as he started the search on his phone for another hookah spot in the area. "The place was so empty it looked like we were going to be their only customers for the entire night. They have some nerve trying to swindle me." he declared while stomping around in a huff.

"Still feeling sour about Vegas after all this time huh?" I teased, concealing my laugh by holding my fist in front of my lips.

"What happened in Vegas?" my brother Selvon inquired with a raised eyebrow.

I couldn't help but titter at the question. Unlike Xavier, I found the experience so cliche it was hilarious. "Xavier and I took a trip to Vegas a couple years back on a whim and, even though we had landed in Sin City around midnight, we agreed that it would be a waste of time to go to our hotel room and sleep. Especially when we were there for the nightlife to begin with. So, we dropped off our things at the hotel and called a taxi to swing us by the nearest club. It happened to have hookah, so of course we ordered some and they set us up in a nice little red booth with cushy seats that we were told came with the hookah. Then after about twenty minutes, some behemoth of a bouncer walked over to us and forced us to pay a fee for sitting in the so-called VIP section by threatening to toss us out if we didn't. I was just going to move but Xavier begrudgingly paid so we could avoid any trouble."

"You guys smoke a lot of hookah, don't you?" My brother's best friend, Terrell, pointed out.

Half embarrassed, I started rubbing the back of my head and smiling like I had been caught with my hand in the cookie jar. "Well, we used to, but I actually haven't touched the stuff in two years."

"Come on! Why is almost every bar closed tonight?" Xavier complained as he continued his search.

I smiled as I watched him pace back and forth while trying to rescue our guy's night out. "Today was going to be an exception, but maybe this is God's way of saying I need to keep these lungs shisha free," I half-joked while patting my chest.

"Wait, it's really been two years already?" Pedro interjected, astonished by how much time had passed. "Seems like just yesterday we were all smoking Special Hookah in your apartment. Why did you even quit?"

Staring up at the night sky, my heart fluttered for a moment. "Well, eventually I realized it wasn't any better than smoking cigarettes every day, and I just wanted to be healthier and live as long as possible for..."

"I found something!" Xavier announced while excitedly pointing at his screen repeatedly. "It's a few miles down the road so we don't have to go very far."

Quickly, he shared the address with us, and we made our way to the two cars we had used to get to that deserted shopping center that housed the less than hospitable hookah joint. Then Xavier raised an age-old question. "Who's riding with who?"

We all looked around at each other for a second, not quite sure of how we should divide the group for this leg of the journey, until our resident teacher gave us the answer.

"You, your brother and Terrell can ride with me this time Ant." Charles offered, beckoning us toward his car. "Can't just stand around here wasting time when there's drank to be drunk and hookah begging to be smoked." he quipped.

Xavier and Pedro nodded in agreement and we all quickly hopped into our respective vehicles and peeled out of the parking lot, rushing to what seemed to be the only other hookah spot in the immediate area that was open for business on a Wednesday night.

What we thought would be a hookah lounge turned out to be a deli style restaurant that also supplied hookah on the side. It was a quaint little dining spot with a dingy, cushioned wall bench that ran along the length of the right wall, and brown, checkered tables placed in front of it that were separated from each other by about two feet. Seemingly impromptu white chairs that appeared to have been snatched straight from a classroom were placed on the opposite side of the tables from the wall, which lent to the homey feel.

We ordered two sets of hookahs, our typical candy flavored shisha that was one of the two main ingredients in our famous Special Hookah, and green apple.

My first drag of smoke felt like a dream long forgotten, and I cherished it like it was my first drink of water after a hard day's work in the sun. I held it in my lungs, and, upon release, watched the clouds of euphoria rise to the ceiling; just like I always used to during our once weekly sessions.

"Is it as good as the first time you smoked after quitting for Madison?" Xavier asked while taking a sip of his fancy artisan soda he had purchased at the counter.

"Way better," I responded with clouds of smoke escaping between my teeth and a look of elation on my face.

Charles gestured for one of the hoses and, before placing it between his lips, unleashed a secret that surprised us all. "You know, I never liked Madison."

I laughed so hard at his bluntness I practically spit out the haze occupying my mouth. When I asked him why he never said anything while I was dating her, he simply said it wasn't his place since he had never met her in person. Based purely on my stories at the time, he didn't like how she seemed to treat me or how her personality mirrored Amanda's, whom he had met and found distasteful.

"Come to think of it, I didn't care for most of the girls in your circle, including Zee." he realized aloud while stroking his chin. "But you know, Neia is really good for you. I can tell you guys really vibe off of each other and pull the best out of one another."

"Well, now I won't know if you're telling the truth unless we break up?" I contested while looking at Xavier and chuckling.

Charles shrugged his shoulders after a few seconds of thought. "You got me there, but I can say I've never lied to you. I just didn't share all of my thoughts before."

I squinted my eyes at Charles, attempting to find holes in his logic that didn't exist. "You win again, Mr. Stewart," I said with a whisper before taking another drag from the hose. "Well, I definitely went through a lot of rough before I found this diamond, so I know she's the one."

"Ain't that the truth" Xavier concurred. "This guy was dating women like there was a bulk sale at Costco before he met her. It got to the point where I started to avoid meeting most of them because I knew they weren't going to stick around for long."

"Hey, that's not true! I just refused to drag a relationship along if I knew it wasn't going to work out in the end. Why waste their time or mine?"

Pedro, who had been scribbling on a napkin, looked up from his spontaneous art piece in order to chime in on the conversation. "So, what made her different from all of the others? It had to be a pretty fun first date."

"Nope." I answered without needing to think for a second. "Our second date was fantastic, but the first was actually one of the worst I had ever been on. She was so late to the restaurant that the only reason I was still there when she arrived was that I had fallen asleep in my car. By the time I woke up, she was pulling in and I was starving so I couldn't think of a reason not to go on with the date. Then after we ate, we drove over to the mall to see a movie and it was so jam packed that it took us an hour to get to the top of the parking garage. To make matters worse, once we got to the top there were no spots left and we were relegated to driving another half hour through the same traffic to reach the bottom. Keep in mind we were in separate cars the whole time, so half of our date took place over the phone as we slogged through that ordeal. After that we agreed to try another theater and chose a random movie that neither of us had heard of."

Pedro looked confused. "And what made you want to see her a second time?"

I mulled over the question for a second, but I didn't have a real answer. "It's hard to explain. I guess for the first time in my entire life, I was able to be unabashedly me with a woman. It was just something about her vibe that told me that I didn't have to hold myself back. For the first time, it felt like I was connecting with a woman, and not just conforming to their desires so they'd stick around. Even after everything that went wrong, we clicked. I wasn't going to let someone like that exit my life without a second date." My mouth twisted into a teasing smirk that was directed at Pedro. "Especially after a certain someone had suggested that maybe there wasn't anyone in this world that could love me."

Pedro winced and rushed to his own defense. "You know I stick my foot in my mouth sometimes! And besides, you said it first. It was early in the morning, and we were swamped getting the lab prepped for the day; I just mindlessly agreed when you were moaning and groaning about potentially having no soul mate!"

We all chortled at Pedro's obvious embarrassment and frantic rebuttal. "I know you didn't mean anything malicious by it, I'm just never going to stop calling you out on it" I said with a hearty laugh and a pat to his shoulder.

The six of us continued chatting and recounting stories in that little delicatessen that moonlighted as a hookah lounge until our coals had turned to ash and the smoke had completely dissipated from the water basin. By the time we had finished, I was exhausted and my throat felt raw from the smoke being reintroduced to my system. But the night was still young, and rest would have to wait.

***

Back in the car, and on route to pick up cheap convenience store booze, I leaned up against the car door and watched the trees lining the road zoom by in the darkness. I wondered what mysteries laid within them and imagined a man dashing alongside our car at superhuman speeds from an unseen and imaginary threat. The drive was going to be less than five minutes, so we hadn't even bothered to play music over the speakers. This suited me fine, since I was having a ball letting my imagination run wild during the short journey.

"Did you get a chance to read that mindset book I got you?" Charles questioned while staring at the road.

"Oh yeah, of course! I actually finished it about a week ago." I responded quickly after being pulled back into reality. "I was still a bit hesitant after hearing you and Neia believed in my dream, but I think that book of yours gave me the final kick in the pants I needed to start writing. I may not know if it will be any good, or even what my style may be, but I'll never know if I don't try."

Charles glanced over at me with a big, slightly cocky, grin. "I'm glad it really helped you bro. It's got some basic concepts, but they can help to put things in perspective. And hey man, I'm telling you, all you need to do is write that first chapter, and things will be easier from there."

I raised an eyebrow in disbelief. "The first chapter, huh? Well, I guess I'm forced to believe my esteemed editor." I peered out onto the open road, noticing a strip of stores had popped up in the distance, signifying our destination wasn't too far off. "By the way, how much did you want to be paid? I'll feel guilty if you get nothing out of this" I added while nervously laughing and praying the price wouldn't be steep.

Charles scrunched his face and snorted uproariously. "Pay? How about you just put in a good word for me to Neia's cute teacher friend and we'll call it even."

I smiled appreciatively at Charles, until the moment was interrupted by the GPS announcing we had arrived at the convenience store. As planned, Charles stopped and we picked up the drinks, but having noticed a donut and ice cream shop on the opposite end of the strip, we forewent the typical snacks like the chips and candy that were available at the store and instead decided to take the short walk to satisfy our growling stomachs with some frozen and fried confections.

While my brother and his friend quickly decided what would appease their appetites and ran to the front of the line to join Xavier and Pedro who were already ordering their own sugary delights, I remained out of line with Charles who stood looking intently at the vividly colored menu strewn across the wall behind the counter.

Thinking back to the book Charles had gifted me and the countless times he had motivated and enlightened me, I felt compelled to admit something I had only ever told my mother the day I had sat crying in my car.

"It's funny Charles, after you left for China I never thought I'd see you again. I was certain you'd have forgotten about a boring guy like me. Then six months later, you messaged me just to recommend a game you thought I'd like. I wish you could have seen how shocked and elated I was that you had proven me wrong once again. Now look at us. You're still advising me like a professor, even though we've been out of college longer than we were in it."

Charles turned to me with a look of shock and slight dismay, "Longer than we were in it? Really?" He looked down at his feet, obviously doing the math in his head. "Hmm, I guess so. Tomorrow is four years on the dot since graduation. We're getting old!" he concluded with a weak laugh. I laughed as well, pointing at Charles and brandishing a smile that screamed "bingo!"

The chuckles died, and Charles pried his eyes away from the menu and looked at me over his shoulder. "So, you really thought you'd never hear from me again?" He asked with a warm but investigative tone in his voice.

I shyly looked away and barely managed to stutter out a meek, "Well yeah." My eyes darted back and forth between him and the menu.

Noticing that I was a bit embarrassed by the confession, Charles continued by saying, "I'll admit, once I came back from China it was hard juggling everyone I knew, but I've never considered you to be someone I should spend less time with. Plus, I look forward to Grilled Cheese Night and our annual camping trips far too much to rid my life of those experiences any time soon." Charles chortled to himself and patted my shoulder before walking to the front of the line, finally having made a decision on what to order.

I remained standing off to the side for a bit, staring at the menu in deep thought, but eventually giving up after being unable to choose which nibbles would best satisfy my sweet tooth. I walked over to the rest of our group, who had already received their orders and were currently stuffing their faces, and sat down in front of Xavier, supporting my head with my hand, and gawking at his box of seasonal donuts. "It's funny, I never imagined that part of my bachelor party would involve getting ice cream and donuts." I mused with a titter while stealing one of Xavier's star shaped goodies.

"Don't tell me you're not having a good time." Xavier pled between sips of his milkshake.

"Quite the opposite. It feels oddly fitting," I leaned in to whisper, "but I can't lie, I'm already feeling tired. How lame is that?"

Xavier, my Best Man, sighed out of relief, "Thank God someone else said it. I thought it was just me!" He confessed.

"We really are a couple of lame-o's aren't we? We haven't even started drinking yet."

"Maybe we burned off all of our wild years early. After you and Tori had broken up we were spending money like trust fund kids. Fancy restaurants, kayaking, indoor skydiving, bar hopping, crossing states just to eat at new restaurants, Vegas; we were really living the crazy bachelor life for a while there." I pointed out.

Xavier winced as an image of all the money we had spent after his heart break flew through his mind. "Damn, we burned through a ton of money being stupid. But I wouldn't trade those good times for anything."

"Neither would I man," I said while scanning the room. Pedro was doodling on a napkin once again, and Charles was shuffling his way toward us with his donuts in hand. Then, once my eyes hit my brother and Terrell guffawing at some video on a phone, nostalgia hit me like a train. Their smiles evoked memories of the simpler days at Mason when we would sit around in our dorms watching mindless videos and laughing like madmen. It took me all the way back to the midnight hangouts with the Eisenhower Crew where we'd play pool and chess until we were delirious. These people that I had met so serendipitously were now not only the best friends I had ever had, but my confidants, colleagues, motivators, and teachers. My adventures with them provided me with more than just the fleeting emotions of happiness and excitement that I had pursued for so long and believed were the key to a fulfilling life. They taught me how to accept who I was, pursue my dreams, and love myself no matter the good or bad that life threw at me at any given moment; they taught me how to be okay. I was proud to call these men my groomsmen and family.

"Neither would I." I repeated once more to myself, thanking God in silence for that one moment in front of the vending machine that made it all possible.

Notes From the Author

The idea for this book was born from the influence of multiple and unlikely sources. From the hilarious Ali Wong's memoir to her daughters, to Michelle Obama's Becoming, I was inspired to create a piece of work for my children that could teach them what they may not have a chance to learn from me. Whether it is because they are too afraid to ask, like I was with my parents, or because God calls me home too soon for me to help them through what may be the most difficult developmental period of their lives.

The book was written over a period of two and a half years, the work officially starting in April of 2019 after I had introduced the concept to my now wife Neia and my good friend Charles as a silly idea I assumed they would dismiss quickly. They believed in me before I had even believed in myself and encouraged me to follow my dreams to be a writer. I will be forever grateful to them, as well as Xavier and Pedro who gave me their full support once I had let them in on the little project.

Knowing how terrible the human mind is at remembering, I chose to sift through all of the resources I could to corroborate my memories. I reviewed old conversations and posts on every social media platform where I still had an active account, old group chats, emails, apartment leases, academic calendars, GMU floor plans, and even weather reports. I also took the time to interview both Xavier and Charles to confirm stories that involved them as well. I chose not to interview anyone else that appears in the story in order to not taint my experience with their perception of events, as (like with everyone) my perception of events is what drove my personal narrative and led me to where I am today. I did my best to recount events accurately, but simply from my point of view.

This story is composed of chronic personal issues and the influence of the events following the night where Lunan approached me at the vending machine. Thus, the tale ends at a point where I feel its direct impact had finally diminished, and too many other factors (whim, working to make ends meet, health, etc) had gained greater influence. Nothing in this book would have occurred the way it did if it weren't for his kindness; whether it was good or bad, it was all a carryover from his decision to ask me how I was doing.

I'd like to conclude by saying that everyone's self-love journey is different, and I don't want my writings to be perceived as a roadmap to solving someone else's problems. Not even by my own children. For that reason, the events between the final two chapters are merely referenced and not fully explained. This is just my story to show that no matter how small our interactions with someone are, and no matter how short the period of time we are in their life may be, we can have a great impact that lasts them a lifetime. So be kind to those you meet, knowing that you may never know where that moment will take them.